Great Lakes Monsters and Mysteries

GREAT LAKES MONSTERS AND MYSTERIES

BRAD BLAIR & TIM ELLIS

Monsters and
mysterious things
that inhabit
this place are not
to be trusted

COVER AND ILLUSTRATIONS BY JASON MCLEOD

Visionary Living Publishing / Visionary Living, Inc.

New Milford, Connecticut

Cover art and illustrations by Jason McLeod.
Cover and interiors designed by John Cheek.

ISBN: 978-1-942157-52-6 (pbk)
ISBN: 978-1-942157-53-3 (epub)

Published by Visionary Living Publishing/ Visionary Living, Inc.
New Milford, Connecticut
www.visionarylivingpublishing.com

Dedication

This book is dedicated to two very special friends:

Rosemary Ellen Guiley, who was an inspiration in our research of worlds beyond the norm, and pushed us outside our comfort zone to become documenters of the paranormal.

Don Hermanson – a pioneer of legend hunting in the Great Lakes region. Friend, teammate, and brother, you remain with us every time we gather to research the unknown.

Contents

Foreword

By Jeff Belanger

Picture one of those perfect summer sundowns, and you're a kid sitting by a campfire on a beachy shore of Lake Superior in Michigan's Upper Peninsula. The fire is starting to crackle as the last golden glow of sunlight bleeds out into the lake's still horizon line to the west. The night air is just cold enough to give you a slight shiver as you move closer to the fire for warmth, sure, but maybe for safety too, as you can't help checking over your shoulder on dark nights like these. When the lake finally turns to a seemingly endless sea of inky black, folks around the fire start talking about strange tales of lake monsters, serpents, hairy upright creatures that stalk the woods, odd lights in the sky, and ghostly apparitions that call out for attention in almost-forgotten places.

A childhood like that may just turn you into a legend-tripping explorer of things that bump and growl in the night, just like Brad Blair and Tim Ellis, two of the most prominent paranormal investigators from the Great Lakes region.

Don't let the term "paranormal investigator" scare you off. This isn't some technical investigative guide, though you'll find plenty of starting points for your own adventures. Consider that long before there's a paranormal investigation, there's a story. Some tale that may sound crazy at first, begs for a closer inspection because somewhere deep inside, you wonder if at least parts of the story may be true. *Great Lakes Monsters and Mysteries* is a collection of just such tales.

I've said before that once you start heading down the rabbit hole, there's no point in stopping halfway. You need to see that journey through. Though Brad and Tim began their paranormal journey by investigating ghosts, they've definitely branched out into all manner of legend and lore, because as it turns out, one man's ghost is another man's demon, is another man's alien, is another man's cryptid, and on and on we go.

Some of these stories have roots that date back millennia, to a time long before European settlers ever gazed upon these giant, freshwater inland seas. There's the Piasa, the Illini people's version of the Thunderbird, and the Singing Sands of Bete Gris on Lake Superior's Keweenaw Peninsula, where a ghostly Indian maiden still calls out for her lost husband.

Other legends were born in more recent times and in more populated centers. Consider the alleged Mothman sightings over Chicago that began in 2017 and continue to this day depending on who you ask, or a vampire reported in Mineral Point, Wisconsin.

From large cities, to remote coves, the Great Lakes cover more than 94,000 square miles of water alone. Add a few miles of inland from there, and millions of residents and visitors, and you have ripe conditions for first-hand accounts of the strange and unexplained to pass into legend as it moves from person-to-person.

Somewhere deep at the root of these accounts sits something primal that connects to the deepest parts of ourselves. Whether you're gazing skyward for winged beasts or unidentified flying ships, or you're looking below water for creatures yet discovered, or even hiking the woods in search of monsters that have been reported for centuries, skeptics-be-damned, Brad and Tim are the right guides to take you inside the legends and introduce you to the witnesses.

However, if you see them running away… try and keep up, or you might just be a chapter in their next book.

Jeff Belanger

Introduction

FROM THE CROWDED STREETS OF CHICAGO TO THE REMOTE WILDERNESS OF MICHIGAN'S UPPER PENINSULA, the Great Lakes region has a history and culture all its own, tied together by its geographic connection to these inland seas. These waterways serve as the center of recreation and commerce for a large segment of the United States' and Canadian populations. They draw visitors from around the world to enjoy their natural beauty and marvel at the great metropolises along their shores. Yet even after centuries of exploration and development, these lakes and their bordering landscapes conceal mysteries and legends, waiting to be explored. During the research and writing of this book, we discovered tales that seemed like those from the pages of a children's book, while others read like horror stories straight out of a Stephen King novel.

The world's largest group of freshwater lakes, what we know today as the Great Lakes: Ontario, Erie, Huron, Michigan, and Superior, was once part of a large ice field during the last glacial period. Roughly 10,000 to 12,000 years ago, this enormous glacier receded, forming the Great Lakes basin. If we chose to forego this scientific explanation, we could jump right into the region's folklore and relate how the Great Lakes were formed by the footprints of the legendary Paul Bunyan. For the sake of this book, even though we are researching legends, we will stick with the glacier story.

With its fertile soil, fresh water, and abundant wildlife, the area was first settled by the earliest of Native American tribes, who thrived off the natural resources offered in the region. These post-ice age inhabitants developed their own culture, complete with deities and mythology, which they passed down orally through generations for thousands of years. Though tribes varied by geographic region and developed their own unique tales, the similarities of supernatural creatures in much of their lore are astounding.

When European explorers arrived in the early years of the 17th century, they were greeted with tales of lake monsters in the depths, sky people and giant birds roaming the atmosphere, spirit beings interacting with the living, and elusive, shape-shifting creatures hiding in the forests.

A steady barrage of settlers followed and brought with them their own legends and folklore, which often intermixed with tribal tales to produce hybrids of Native American and European folklore. But what about the stories that remained pure; the encounters which were said to be more than mere myth?

When French voyageurs took to the lakes to move their caches of furs to the nearest trading post, every tribe they encountered warned them of massive, serpent-like creatures that inhabited the waterways. More than a few recounted supposedly true sightings of lake monsters. Sightings continue right up through modern day as sailors who earn their living on Great Lakes freighters still report unknown creatures of the depths.

Today, Bigfoot hunters search for the hairy wild men of these Midwest forests, paranormal researchers attempt to contact spiritual entities in crowded cities, and ufologists examine reports of interaction with alien "sky people" and their vessels. The mysteries and legends of the region continue to evolve with the times.

Although many of these sightings have similar counterparts throughout the world, those of the Great Lakes region possess their own unique back-stories and characteristics that won't be found elsewhere on the planet. Whether based in ancient legend or bizarre flesh and blood encounters, these tales continue to be told. Those brave enough to explore their origins often find themselves caught up in the boundaries between legend and reality. That is exactly where we hope these pages will take you.

Sea Serpents and Mermaids

THE CRISP MORNING AIR ENLIVENED THE YOUNG COUPLE, embracing them as they emerged from their tent at the makeshift campsite they had established near the loch the prior evening. The summer sun would warm the surrounding forest well before noon, but they planned on finishing their early morning hike before the woodland trails became muggy and mosquito infested.

As the two made their way to the lochside path, the fog rolled back from the water, dissipating with the first rays of sunlight. The dawn revealed the natural beauty which drew them to spend their vacation here in the north country. Stopping to take in the sights and sounds of the waterfront, they noticed a ripple in the surface. Not more than twenty yards from them a series of humps emerged from the otherwise still water. The startled couple stared in silence as what appeared to be a serpentine head rose from the water, turned, and peered with saucer-sized eyes in their direction, then dropped back into the depths.

This type of encounter may seem commonplace when sharing stories of Loch Ness, alleged home of the world's most famous sea serpent,

Nessie. However, the above described encounter did not take place in the Highlands of Scotland, but at another famous loch, on the other side of the world, Loch Superior, or Lake Superior as we call it here in the Western Hemisphere. These are the tales I was told growing up on the far eastern shore of Lake Superior in Sault Ste. Marie, Michigan, where the lake joins the St. Mary's River to connect to her four southern sisters. How many of these "fish tales" were legitimate sightings versus creations to be told at beachside campfires will always be debatable, but if the land and skies of the region hold their own mysteries, the depths of her seas most definitely do as well.

And why wouldn't Lake Superior, known to the original Ojibwa inhabitants as *Gitche Gumi*, be home to an unknown creature (or creatures) of mythical proportion? If you took the surface area of Loch Ness, which is approximately 22 square miles, and placed it over Lake Superior, you would be able to fit around 1,441 Loch Nesses on top of this largest great lake. Adding in the fact that the five connected Great Lakes contain more than six-quadrillion gallons of fresh water (give or take a couple gallons), you have a massive underwater ecosystem that will conceal all sizes of aquatic and amphibious beings.

Each of these "inland seas" has produced many monster sightings over the centuries, beginning with early Native American encounters and continuing up to modern day reports. Could the same aquatic cryptid haunt all five of the Great Lakes? Although a solitary large animal could easily travel undetected between three of the five lakes, it would either have to "lock" through the shipping canal in Sault Ste. Marie, Michigan, to get to or from Lake Superior, or traverse the Welland Canal to move between Lakes Ontario and Erie. Both routes seem unlikely. Reports of sightings note creatures of vastly differing characteristics and sizes. A single creature would have to travel overwhelming distances to appear in all these vast bodies of water. Therefore, we assume that each of these lakes houses their own unique unknowns, lurking in their cold fresh depths.

Lake Ontario

Being the westernmost of the Great Lakes, Lake Ontario is isolated from other major waterways by the Welland Canal to the west and the St. Lawrence Seaway with its lock system to the east. With these barriers in place, any large creatures in its waters must be isolated to this single lake and must have been since these systems were put in place.

Ontario's monster seems to have roamed its waters long before either nautical barrier was erected. Sightings of serpentine creatures in Lake Ontario predate the arrival of Europeans by centuries. The Seneca tribe passed down the legend of Gaasyendietha, a dragon which fell to earth in the form of a meteor and made its home in the deepest areas of the lake, shape-shifting into other creatures as the need arose.

French explorer Jacques Cartier may have been the first European to encounter Gaasyendietha. When he sailed across Lake Ontario in the 1500s, he described sighting a massive "finned snake" breaking the water line near his vessel, frightening the crew, and putting all men on high alert. He may have been the first, but he would not be the last.

As immigrant settlers began making their homes along the shorelines of the lake, sightings of a strange creature became more prevalent. In fact, throughout the 1800s stories of lake monsters were quite common in the newspapers of the day. On August 14th, 1829, the *Kingston Gazette* of Kingston, Ontario, reported the following encounter:

> Lake Serpent- A neighbor informs us, that his children (from 10 to 14 years old) were a few days since playing on the lake shore, near the mouth of the 10 mile creek, Grantham, when suddenly appeared in the water a few feet from the spot where they were standing, a hideous water snake, or serpent, of prodigious dimensions. According to their account, it must have been twenty or thirty feet in length, with a head ten or fifteen inches in diameter, and warts or bunches on it. In giving the alarm, it immediately turned and disappeared. This, we believe, is not the first one of the kind that has been seen in Lake Ontario: and from what we can learn, there can be no doubt of the existence of such monsters in our inland seas.

Reports continued to pour in through the years. In July of 1833, a Captain Kellogg of the schooner *Polythermus* reported to the *Oswego Palladium* of Oswego, New York, an encounter with a serpentine creature in the lake. He described the beast as resembling the mast of a vessel, until it began to take motion toward the schooner. At closer observation, Kellogg noted it as about 175 feet long and dark blue in color with brown spots and having the "circumference of a flour barrel." The captain claims the entire crew observed the creature for a full fifteen minutes before it moved off towards the St. Lawrence.

Sightings continued to find their way into newsprint in every decade throughout the 1900s, from both the Canadian and American sides of the lake, with varying descriptions including horse-sized eyes, stiff bristles covering the body, and even a claim the creature had one eye in the center of its head and sported a pair of antlers! With the vast differences in eyewitness accounts – even allowing only a minimum to be factual – one might believe that even the smallest of the Great Lakes may be home to more than one species of "aquatic unknown."

Lake Erie

Lake Erie, fourth largest of the Great Lakes, has also logged its share of anomalous aquatic creature reports. Encounters became so common that inhabitants of the lakeside communities named the sea monster "Bessie." Although sightings of a giant serpent in the lake occur on what seems a semiregular basis, Bessie is far from being a contemporary urban legend, as her history reaches far back to the earliest settlers of Erie's shores.

The first European credited with sailing Lake Erie was a French-Canadian explorer named Louis Jolliet, who came to the area in 1669, looking to establish trade with the local band of Iroquois natives who inhabited the region. The Iroquois had great respect for the lake, as it provided sustenance in the form of the many species of fish and marine mammals. But they taught their young to fear the mighty Oniare (pronounced own-yar-eh) alleged to live in the coldest depths of Erie. The Oniare was said to be a dragon-like horned serpent which had a vile, poisonous breath. If Iroquois fishermen paddled too far out in their canoes, they ran the risk of the Oniare flipping the boat and devouring all who were ejected into the water. These tales were passed on to Jolliet, a friendly warning that his larger vessel was still no match for the might of the great horned serpent.

The weather is known to turn quickly on the lakes. How many native fishermen in their early canoes capsized as the result of a fast-moving storm and drowned, never to return to the tribe? These tragedies would likely have contributed to the continued belief in a great creature hunting those who dared to venture into its domain.

The first modern sighting of a sea serpent in Lake Erie can be traced back to 1793 when the captain of the schooner *Felicity*, while transporting trade goods across the lake, logged a report of a monstrous beast he estimated to be longer than 17 feet. The creature rose out of the water near Middle Bass

Island, just north of Ohio, startling both captain and crew. Although reports have been filed in almost all areas of the lake through the years, this area of Ohio shoreline seems to be Bessie's preferred habitat.

In 1817 a rash of appearances were reported to authorities, mainly from the crews of schooners traveling the southern end of Erie. Another wave of reports found their way to local newspapers nearly every summer of the 1890s.

One of the more remarkable accounts described two brothers' close encounter in May 1877, with a twenty to thirty-foot creature writhing in agony on the shore. The siblings decided to fetch a rope in the hopes of dragging the creature up onto land. When they returned, as so often seems to be the case in reports like this one, the beast had vanished, presumably back into the depths.

One of the lengthiest observances of Bessie occurred in 1896 at Crystal Beach, near Fort Erie, Ontario, where on May 5th of that year a group of beachgoers described viewing a roughly 30-foot creature, with a head like a dog and a pointy tail, circling in the waters for nearly 45 minutes. Following this sighting, The *Buffalo Courier* reported "The serpent of the Great Lakes has been seen so many times now, by sane, sober and truthful people, that he who sees it hereafter need have no timidity about mentioning the fact."

And indeed, many people have continued to report sightings of the creature to both the local authorities and the Coast Guard. In 1993, a group of businessmen in Huron, Ohio, offered a reward of more than $100,000 for definitive proof of Bessie's existence. The reward was never claimed, but the offer attracted monster hunters and curiosity seekers to the area as well as much media attention and brought in a flood of tourist dollars to the lakeside community.

Whether or not there is any validity to these many "fish tales," Bessie has become so ingrained in the region's folklore that she has left an indelible mark on the area's pop culture. Cleveland has a professional American Hockey League team named the Lake Erie Monsters, beer lovers can enjoy a Lake Erie Monster IPA available through the Great Lakes Brewing Company, and in 2017 luxury watch maker Shinola began producing a high end dive watch branded the Lake Erie Monster; all signs that the beast is not only alive and well in the hearts and minds of Lake Erie's seaside citizens, but also in the cash registers of the area's retail and tourist trade.

Lake Huron

Thought to be the first of the Great Lakes traversed by European explorers, Lake Huron, second largest of the lakes by surface area, has known its share of nautical anomalies through the ages. Originally referred to as La Mer Douce, or Sweetwater Sea, by the French, Huron played a crucial role in the fur trading days of the early voyageurs, trappers who traded with the indigenous peoples of the area, and heavily influenced the first European communities of the region.

The voyageurs' initial exposure to La Mer Douce's fierce aquatic inhabitants came from the legends of the Ojibwe people who made their homes along the Huron shore. These tales told of a mighty lake creature – not a serpent in this case but a cryptid feline – who roamed Huron from its den near the northern channel. Mishebeshu, the Great Water Lynx, was said to make its home near where the Serpent River, located at the top of the lake between Sault Ste. Marie and Sudbury, Ontario, flows into Huron. As with the maritime monsters of the southern Great Lakes, legend attributed the deaths of fishermen to this creature, lying in wait to capsize canoes and make meals out of the unlucky occupants.

Roaming the waters of the North Country, where the surface of the lake freezes in the winter months, Mishebeshu was also blamed for the loss of poor souls who ventured out onto the ice and were swallowed up by the lake on occasions when the unstable surface cracked and gave way, a tragic fate not uncommon amongst those eager to explore the partially frozen water before the ice was dense enough to support their weight.

Although native legend warns of a giant cat in Huron, most cryptid reports from modern seafarers tend to conform to the sightings of her southern sisters: a large, serpent-like creature roaming the trade routes. Just such a report was filed in October of 1938 when a fishing crew from Sarnia, Ontario, spotted a 30-foot serpent splashing in the water near their vessel, frightening the captain enough to call an early end to the day's work, and race his ship to the nearest port.

In spite of the serpentine appearance (assuming it to be a cold-blooded creature), a bulk of the reported Huron sightings come from the colder waters at the far northern end of the lake, as was the encounter one pleasant July night in 1847. As dusk descended on Mackinac Island, Michigan, a group of men sitting near the lakeshore at Mission Point were startled by the appearance of what was described as "an enormous sea serpent elevating its head, undulating its humps, and floating 'many a rood' upon the translucent strait." The beast was again spotted off the Island 142 years later in 1989, when a woman reported observing a lengthy creature with its head sticking roughly two feet out of the water as it swam between the island and the mainland of St. Ignace.

Just south of Mackinac, in the waters off Cheboygan, Michigan (a fairly easy commute for a creature of this purported size), a very similar beast has been reported throughout the years. On an early fall night in 1975, a local couple spotted what they believed to be a 40-foot serpent swimming just feet away from their dock. The following June, the *Grand Rapids Press* ran an article alleging that another Cheboygan resident had viewed not one, but two of these creatures flailing through the waters near his home. A county sheriff's deputy reported one such animal on the same evening and conceded that he could not even attempt to identify the beast. These reports all came from the same roughly 10 mile stretch of Lake Huron waterfront area surrounding the city.

One of the most compelling creature sightings took place not in Lake Huron proper, but at the northern end of the St. Mary's River, which connects Huron to Lake Superior, in an area much closer to Superior than Huron. In the 1960s, a family on Sugar Island watched as a large scaly beast swam back and forth near the family's waterfront property. The beast seemed to be making continuous circles in the area, submerging and reappearing for a period of approximately ten minutes. Although many monster enthusiasts attribute this sighting to Pressie, the Lake Superior serpent, it would be hard to fathom a creature of this purported size navigating through the shallow rapids at Sault Ste. Marie, much less going unnoticed doing so, or secretly entering the Soo Locks canal system to make its way south into the St. Mary's. It is more conceivable that the beast made its way north (especially considering the number of sightings near the Straits of Mackinac, relatively close to the southern end of the St. Mary's River) and hit a dead end at the Sault Rapids. Given the great width of the nearly 75-mile-long St. Mary's, the creature could easily avoid detection by cargo ships or fishing vessels on its sojourn to the northern border and back.

Lake Michigan

Although connected to the monster-rich Lake Huron in the north by the nearly five-mile-wide waterway at the Straits of Mackinac, Lake Michigan may have the least amount of "sea serpent" sightings of all five lakes, yet is home to some of the greatest of Great Lake mysteries, dating back even farther than the formation of the lakes themselves.

In the summer of 2007, Mark Holley, a professor of underwater archeology, undertook an expedition to scan the floor of Lake Michigan for undiscovered shipwrecks. With an estimated 1,500 wrecks on the lake, many of which have never been located, searching for the remains of doomed vessels is a prominent task of both professional archaeologists and amateur wreck hunters alike. While searching the lakebed off Grand Traverse Bay, Holley's equipment registered an anomaly which turned out to be something much more mysterious than a long-lost schooner.

Upon further exploration, it was revealed that the scan had discovered a megalithic stone structure from a time prior to the formation of the Great Lakes. The huge stones assembled in the underwater circle were estimated to weigh 50 tons each and were assumed to have been placed there by early humans. Although dating the structure is quite difficult, one stone found in the immediate area showed an engraving of what appears to be a mastodon, an animal believed to have gone extinct 10,000 years ago. Taking into account that the lakes were believed to have formed at the end of the last glacial period (around 14,000 years ago) and the world-famous Stonehenge rock circle of England is estimated to have been constructed around 5,000 years ago, the Lake Michigan circle would be more than twice as old as its famous British cousin!

The discovery of this Lake Michigan Stonehenge opened a whole new world of mysteries and raised many questions. What ancient society assembled the massive structures? How could humans move stones of such magnitude without the aid of advanced tools? What purpose did the site serve? How long prior to the Ice Age which formed the lakes was it erected? Much like the Stonehenge of England, many theories may be advanced, yet definitive answers may never be revealed. For now, the Lake Michigan Stonehenge remains an eerie, silent monument to a long-forgotten people, resting out of view at the bottom of the lake.

Farther south, a plethora of strange events over the years defined the area now considered the most mysterious region of the Great Lakes, The Lake Michigan Triangle. The triangle extends from Manitowoc, Wisconsin, in the west, across to Ludington, Michigan in the east and down to its southern point at Benton Harbor, Michigan. This section of the lake has been home to a vast array of anomalous events: disappearing planes, missing persons, and strange light phenomena, to name just a few.

The earliest triangle mystery to be brought to public attention dates back to 1891, when the 132-foot, three-masted schooner *Thomas Hume* set sail on a northbound route across Lake Michigan. Having emptied her cargo of lumber in Chicago she was on the way to her homeport of Muskegon, Michigan, sailing in concert with a sister ship from the fleet, the similarly ill-fated *Rouse Simmons*, which would achieve legendary status itself as the doomed Christmas Tree Ship (more on that later). Sailing was smooth at the outset; however, the signs of an oncoming storm grew more visible as the empty vessels advanced.

Fearing the squalls, which were a threat to all maritime traffic, the *Simmons* turned tail and sailed back to Chicago to await the passing of the coming storm. The *Hume* continued into the inclement weather front toward Muskegon, a port it would never reach. When it failed to arrive at its estimated time, rescue vessels were dispatched to search for the ship. Nothing was found; neither wreckage nor any trace of the *Hume's* six-man crew was anywhere to be seen.

Much speculation surrounded the fate of the *Hume*. Did the storm, although not severe by Great Lakes standards, overcome the vessel? Had it been struck by a larger ship and sent to a watery grave? Some conjectured that the crew had hidden the ship, repainted it, and were now sailing under a new name, an early act of grand theft! As any old sailor could tell you, it is maritime superstition that renaming a ship is bad luck, yet the *Hume* had been launched in 1870 as the *H.C. Albrecht*, so the belief that a curse had been wrought with its renaming was prevalent amongst the old salts of the day. Had such a malediction brought about the doom of the missing vessel?

The mystery of the *Hume* would endure for 117 years, until 2005, when a ship discovered at the bottom of Lake Michigan was positively identified as the missing *Thomas Hume*. The wreck startles divers to this day, as the *Hume* is not scattered in pieces or laid on its side on the lakebed, as one may expect a ship taken by a storm to be, but simply rests right side up, as if a giant hand had snatched the ship from the surface and pulled it down to its final resting place. No human remains were ever recovered, and what actually sank the *Hume* remains a mystery.

Another unfortunate maritime disaster of the triangle occurred in 1921 when the two-masted schooner *Rosa Bell* was discovered capsized 42 miles east of Milwaukee. When examined by the Coast Guard, it appeared a larger vessel had rammed the ship; however, no other ships reported an accident or went missing at the time. None of the 11 crew members of the schooner were heard from again, and no human remains were ever discovered.

Possibly the most mysterious case to come out of the Lake Michigan Triangle involves the disappearance of Captain George R. Donner of the freighter *O.M. McFarland*. On the evening of April 28, 1937, after the stressful task of navigating his vessel through a treacherous spring ice field where a wrong move could damage or even sink the ship (think *Titanic*), Captain Donner retired to his cabin for some well-earned rest. After several hours, one of the crew members went to inform the captain that they were nearing port. When Captain Donner failed to answer the call to return to duty, the crew feared he may have suffered some malady, and his second-in-command ordered the men to break down the door to his cabin. What those sailors found would become one of the greatest maritime mysteries of all time. The cabin door was locked from the inside with no other egress available, yet the room lay empty. Captain Donner was nowhere to be found, nor would he ever be seen again. Wild speculation raged as to the whereabouts of the captain, but no rational explanation was ever put forth. Captain Donner had simply vanished into thin air, another victim of the triangle.

Sailing vessels and cargo ships were not the only transports to meet their doom in this cursed region of the lakes. On June 23rd, 1950, Northwest Airlines flight 2501 was making its daily run from New York to Seattle when it radioed in requesting permission to descend to a lower altitude. Shortly thereafter, the plane vanished from radar, with its last known location being approximately 18 miles northwest of Benton Harbor, Michigan.

Despite aviation authorities' knowledge of the flight path, the location of flight 2501 when it disappeared from radar, and the discovery of some personal belongings of known passengers, the plane itself has never been located. Adding to the strangeness of the disappearance, two hours following the final communication from the crew, two police officers reported observing an unidentifiable red light hovering over the area of the lake where the plane was presumed to have gone down. According to the officers' statements, the light was visible for approximately ten minutes before shooting off into the sky.

The disappearance of flight 2501 with all 58 passengers marked the deadliest crash in American aviation history at that point in time. Speculation for the cause of the crash ranges from a possible electrical storm in the area to a collision with a UFO, feeding the rumors that a secret extraterrestrial base, presumably located at the bottom of Lake Michigan, causes much of the chaos which occurs in the region.

As it turns out, there have been a great many UFOs and USOs (Unidentified Submerged Objects) reported in the area of the triangle, with some individuals claiming to have observed these objects entering or exiting the lake. In 2008, an Indiana man was spending a day at the beach with some friends on the southern shore of Lake Michigan when he viewed a round, white flying object that hovered for a period, then flew directly into the lake, disappearing into the depths. In March of 2010, a passenger on a plane flying over Milwaukee reported viewing a large, extremely bright light, followed by two smaller lights, moving under the surface of Lake Michigan, heading in a direct, adjacent path to each other. These are just two of the many claims made by people believing they have witnessed unidentified craft operating within the depths of the lake, craft which some believe have a direct correlation with the phenomena associated with the Lake Michigan Triangle.

And of course, we can't move past the waters of Lake Michigan without encountering a sea serpent or two. Back in the 1800s when headlines of these nautical nuisances were selling papers for lakeside tabloids on her sister lakes, Lake Michigan journalists were also hot on the cryptid cases. An 1893 *Chicago Tribune* article related the sighting of a large serpentine creature by military officers posted at Fort Sheridan, Illinois. It claimed the men were shaken so badly they "signed a pledge to let liquor alone," which leads to speculation as to the condition of these two officers at the time of their sighting. Another article from the same time period told of a fisherman near Milwaukee who witnessed two 50-foot lake creatures frolicking near his vessel. The spectacle unnerved the mariner enough that he avoided returning to the lake for several days. However, fishing being his main means of income, he overcame this apprehension when the need for a paycheck arose.

Sea monster sightings from Michigan's depths are not limited to the newsprint of days gone by, however. In the summer of 2019, video footage recorded off a pier in South Haven, Michigan, by a stationary camera set to observe the local lighthouse, appears to have captured a large creature swimming in the area of the South Haven beacon. The 52 seconds of video was posted online and soon talk of mermaids, sea snakes, and ancient reptiles swirled around the controversial footage. One area resident claimed it was nothing more than a tarp that had blown into the water due to the high winds that day. On July 4th, the *MLive* online news service reported, "Whatever it is, it appears to poke its head out of the water before slinking its way toward the pier. After stopping underneath it for a few seconds, it jumps back into the water quickly." Sea monster or missing tarp; either way, the footage is compelling to view, and marks one more entry into the ongoing mysteries of Lake Michigan.

Lake Superior

Measuring roughly 31,700 square miles by surface area, about the size of the entire state of Maine, Superior is the world's largest freshwater lake. This northernmost of the Great Lakes holds more water than the other four lakes combined, making it an easy place for an aquatic cryptid to hide.

Gitchi Gumi, or Big Sea as it was known to the Native Americans who called the region home for centuries prior to the coming of the Europeans, was both revered and feared by the early inhabitants. Many native legends surround the waters of Superior and the creatures thought to inhabit them.

Among the fierce beings believed to traverse Superior's waters was Mishi-Ginebig, the great horned serpent, which lived in the depths and devoured any unsuspecting humans who were unfortunate enough to venture near its hungry jaws. Although mortal men could not hope to defeat the creature, it did have one sworn enemy, the Thunderbird, who could kill the serpent from the sky by firing thunderbolts at it. Envisioning the sight of the lake rising up in turmoil as a thunderstorm covered the area, it is easy to imagine where a great battle between creatures of the water and sky would be conceived.

Another bizarre being said to roam Superior was the great water lynx, Mishipeshu. Mishipeshu was depicted as having the head and body of a great cat, with spikes running down its back and horns adorning its head. This mythical beast held a specific role to the people of the Lake

Superior region; he was guardian of the copper. It was said that anyone Mishipeshu caught attempting to steal from the large copper deposits along the shores of Gitchi Gumi would suffer a horrendous death, often from drowning or shipwreck, and always some form of water-related fatality. Depictions of Mishipeshu can be viewed to this day in the form of ancient pictographs, which still exist on stones along areas of Superior's rustic shoreline.

Easily one of the most intriguing and cross-culture aquatic creatures of native lore is the Nibinabe, known in most seafaring cultures as a mermaid or merman. Believed to be a spiritual being, legend held that bad luck would befall anyone foolish enough to try capturing or inflicting harm on these half-human, half-fish, ethereal hybrids. In May of 1782, voyageur Venant St. Germain spotted just such a creature from his shoreline campsite near Isle Royale, Michigan. It was near dusk when he and his companions watched from the beach as the merman surfaced around 75 yards offshore. St. Germain described it as having the upper body of a child-sized human. As the story goes, the bewildered voyageur grabbed his rifle to fire a shot at the creature, but was pushed off balance by an accompanying Ojibwe woman who warned of the perils such an action would bring to not just St. Germain, but to everyone present. Venant spent the rest of his life recounting that evening, including relating the tale in a sworn testimony in 1812 in front of a Canadian court.

The award for most renowned of Superior's sea-beasts has to go to her own serpent, Pressie. Named for some of the more up close sightings near the Presque Isle River, Pressie is said to range anywhere between 30 to 75 feet in length, depending on the report, which may suggest more than one of these creatures swim the depths of Superior.

Maritime sightings of a serpentine sea-beast in Superior date back to the late 1850s, after the construction of the Soo Locks Shipping Canal opened the lake to a new boom of commercial traffic. As schooners flooded the north to expedite trade in furs, fish, copper, and lumber, tales of Pressie quickly spread amongst mariners.

Many of the best early sightings occurred in the mid-1890s when she seemed to make her home in the area of the Shipwreck Coast, a region of Lake Superior shoreline running across Michigan's Upper Peninsula from Whitefish Point in the east to Munising in the west. The crews of two different steamers sighted a large serpent near Whitefish Point in 1894, and

13

the following year the same creature reportedly followed a ship past the point for some distance. Sightings would continue along this coastline for many years to come, as Pressie was spotted by fishermen near Munising in 1930, and in 1981 was encountered by five siblings playing on a beach in the same area.

Pressie sightings seem to arrive in clusters in different areas, but she is far from territorial, assuming it is one creature and not an entire population of inland sea serpents roaming the largest of the lakes. She has made her presence known in nearly every region of Superior, from being sighted in the west by a yacht crew off of Duluth in the late 1800s to recent encounters by fishermen in the far eastern area near Point Iroquois in Michigan's Upper Peninsula.

Taking into account the size and depth of this underwater playground, catching a glimpse of any of Gitchi Gumi's undocumented inhabitants seems unlikely at best, but for those who've encountered them and lived to tell the tale, even the largest of lakes may be too small for comfort!

If you think it requires an enormous body of water such as these five Great Lakes to lay claim to being an aquatic cryptid playground, think again. Smaller lakes of the area, including the likes of Lake Nipissing in Ontario, Michigan's Torch Lake, and the dammed up Lake Koshkonong of Wisconsin, and numerous other inland lakes of the region proudly lay claims to their own unique aquatic monstrosities.

Assuming the vast numbers of Lake Monster reports are not the result of mass hallucinations or overactive imaginations, what are witnesses seeing in these landlocked freshwater lakes? I reached out to an expert in the field of Marine Biology, Dr. Sheanna Steingass, to get her opinion on what may lurk in these depths: "The possibility of a large undescribed lake monster in the Great Lakes is pretty unlikely," Dr. Steingass speculated. "No marine mammals exist in these types of habitat in North America. The large expanses of freshwater in the Great Lakes could provide home for large individuals of many fish species, including sturgeons, American eel, pike, and gar that are all capable of creating large disturbances on the water while feeding or spawning. The emergence of new eDNA analysis methods means that this new scientific technique could provide a definitive answer regarding the presence of these iconic cryptids."

So, are seasoned mariners mistaking large fish or eels for 75-foot serpents? Might a mermaid viewed from a distance actually be a large otter or similar marine mammal surfacing to survey its surroundings? Or could there be more to the vast expanse of waters that make up the inland seas known as the Great Lakes? Their depths hide the wrecks of thousands of doomed ships, lost sailors, and mysterious antiquities. Could there also be a long-forgotten species or two, waiting to once again break the surface?

Great Lakes UFO Sightings and Encounters

On a crisp, late fall afternoon in 1993, the United States Coast Guard buoy tender *Sundew* was making its way from Wisconsin on the far western part of Lake Superior. They were maneuvering through a group of islands known as the Apostle Islands on the northern tip of the state. What should have been a routine trip for the ship and her crew was anything but on this day. On deck, a watchman and two crew members noticed a mysterious object in the sky. Trying to figure out what this thing was, the watchman immediately radioed the pilothouse to ask if they saw anything on the radar. "No" was the answer that came back. Smooth sailing was the report, according to the radar.

These trained men realized that they were watching an Unidentified Flying Object about 300 to 500 feet in size, with four rotating lights. The watchman now called for the captain to join them. By the time the captain was able to get to the men on deck, the object had disappeared, but not before three military men witnessed it for close to a half-hour.

Another thirty minutes would pass before it was time for the next watchman to take his post. As he approached, the three men who were still there, still carefully watching the horizon, shared the story with him.

Soon the news spread throughout the ship, and a handful of sailors assembled around the watchman's post. Seven trained sailors were now chatting and watching the skies carefully as the ship continued east into Lake Superior. That's when the UFO appeared again, as quickly as it did the first time.

This time, seven sets of eyes were all watching the same object follow them through the Big Lake. The sailors called the captain to the deck again. Not at all happy to be drawn from his cabin a second time, the captain approached with a stern face. But soon, his expression changed to a puzzled, almost frightened look. Now, he was witnessing the very object he had heard the scuttle over, the past hour or so on the ship.

The captain quickly radioed ahead to the closest Coast Guard base in Sault Ste. Marie, Michigan. He was sure they were witnessing drills or exercises in the area. Flairs, pyros, lights from planes; these had to be the explanations for what the eight men were observing. The radio transmission came back for Sector Sault. Negative. No exercises were taking place, either in the United States or in Canada. There should be nothing in their vicinity. Both Sector Sault, and *Sundew's* radars were still showing NOTHING in their area. Shortly after, the craft vanished, or "sped off," as some witnesses reported, never to be seen by the crew of the *Sundew* again.

What was in the sky that night over Lake Superior, seemingly following a United States Coast Guard vessel? Stories like this litter the files of UFO organizations in the Great Lakes Region. When those stories come from people in positions of respect and trust, such as the military, law enforcement, clergy, doctors, and professors, we tend to listen a little more closely. That's not to take away from any man, woman, or child who has reported and shared a story of a UFO encounter, who may not fall under one of those titles. No matter who steps forward to share their UFO encounter, one thing is for sure, the Great Lakes Region is home to some of the most notable and unusual cases of UFO sightings.

A *USA Today* article from the summer of 2019 ranked the states based on UFO sightings between 2001 and 2015. The numbers came from The National UFO Reporting Center. The eight states that border the Great Lakes Region rank respectably in the country for the amount of UFO sightings. Well, we won't mention the two states who seem to be lacking a bit. Let's blame that on too much cheese and bad football in their diets. By number of sightings the rankings were:

- Pennsylvania 5th
- New York 6th
- Illinois 8th
- Michigan 9th
- Ohio 10th
- Indiana 15th
- Wisconsin 21st
- Minnesota 23rd

Of the states that make up the Great Lakes Region, five of them rank in the top ten in the nation for reported UFO sightings, making this area a hotbed for little greens or bigger greys to be walking around. Why has this part of the country become Disney World for visitors from other planets? Could it be the natural makeup of the Great Lakes being easily seen and used as a kind of map when approaching from space? A place on the planet that looks like no other, and easy to find in the approach to the marble known as earth?

Or, maybe the answer lies not within the skies, but below the surface of The Great Lakes themselves. Unidentified Submersible Objects, or USOs, are a phenomenon that's all over the pages of sailors' logbooks since man started crossing the oceans to discover new land. Mysterious craft are reported to plunge into the waters deep, never to be seen again. Then too, there are reports of ships flying out of the seas and straight into the clouds. Christopher Columbus witnessed a disc-shaped object plummeting from the sky and into the sea. Was it possible he saw a USO on his way to the New World?

The vast expanse and depth of the Great Lakes could very well conceal craft or hide an underwater base. Ranging from 1,333 feet to 2,100 feet, the Great Lakes have plenty of real estate for some extra-terrestrial squatters to make a home without paying their fair share of taxes.

One story of a possible underground base, or at the very least, a crazy underwater anomaly, concerns the west end of Lake Superior, in the waters of Isle Royale. This area is rich with some of the purest copper. It is sacred to the Native Americans, who refer to it as Minong. This story also concerns the same part of Lake Superior where the crew of *Sundew* had their extraordinary experience.

Isle Royale is an island located in northwest Lake Superior, near the Canadian border but part of the State of Michigan. The island, plus about 450 adjacent islands and the surrounding waterways, make up the Isle Royal National Park. The area has long been a place of interest for historians trying to re-write the history books as to who truly set foot in the Great Lakes area first. Carbon dating shows that ancient mining took place in the region over 6,500 years ago! We explore this very subject in another story in this book, titled *The Newberry Stone*.

During an extensive historical research project around Isle Royale, Google Earth was used to get an aerial view of a specific area known as Cargo Cove. The research and footage from Google Earth revealed an ancient discovery. Deep beneath the surface of Lake Superior, on the lake floor, a large anomaly was found, one that surely did not fit into the surrounding landscape.

The structure is approximately four miles off the northern shore of Isle Royale, and only a half-mile from the Canadian/American border, in about 500 feet of water. It measures three miles long, with the broadest part two miles wide. One of the more exciting features is the uniform wall all around the structure, which appears to measure 250 feet in height. There is a quarter mile-wide opening on the northwest side. For the past six years, study and research on the new, ancient discovery have been going on with no more answers today than the day it was discovered.

However, through all the studies, six theories have surfaced as to what this landmark could be. One of those theories is a USO base! One other interesting fact about this find is that around the same time of its discovery, Google Earth found a remarkably similar anomaly beneath the water surface just off Malibu. This is another sacred area to the Native Americans with identical mystical beliefs for the lands and water surrounding it.

Mysteries surrounding UFOs and water have long been written about since authors started telling stories of the Bermuda Triangle. However, the Great Lakes has its own Devil's Triangle. As discussed in the Sea Creatures chapter, Lake Michigan's "Devilish" place is known as The Lake Michigan Triangle, a place where ships, men, and planes have gone missing for no logical reason.

Why would aliens build bases in the bottom of the Great Lakes or even the oceans? The answer seems an easy one. Would you want to travel thousands of light-years away and then turn around and come back? Or would you build a camp and stay close when studying the human race and all of its flaws? And where better to create a camp than in the very depths of our own oceans and lakes, which are as foreign to us as space itself? The answer seems simple now, right?

I recently had a chance to sit down and speak with Bill Konkolesky, the State Director of the Michigan Chapter of the Mutual UFO Network, also known as MUFON. In just a few minutes' conversation with Bill, I found out just how passionate and well versed he is on UFOs and their impact on the Great Lakes region. His respect for the field is unparalleled. I wanted to speak with Bill particularly on a case that happened along the shores of Lake Michigan back in March of 1994. It was during this interview that Bill shared a fantastic story that took place over Lake Huron in 1975. But first, the Lake Michigan UFO event of 1994.

March 8th, 1994 would become known as the beginning of a barrage of UFO sightings that would span weeks, but the night of the 8th would be the evening most remember and talk about today. Over 300 witnesses would come forward to report what they saw in the sky that night, including law enforcement and radar operators.

Over 200 miles along the Lake Michigan shoreline, the phones of local police stations started to ring non-stop. Reports of strange lights in the sky, moving all over the place, was the same story heard from one phone call to another. In the early stages of the calls, the dispatchers are noticeably flippant about the calls, and almost sound annoyed having to take the information. As the calls increase, they start to tell callers that radio towers are to blame for the strange lights in the sky. The calls don't stop, and now the dispatchers are beginning to wonder themselves.

Who made the first phone call that night, we will probably never know. But the Graves family of Holland, Michigan, became the most remembered as it was their report that finally prompted dispatch to send an officer to investigate. Here is what Bill Konkolesky had to say regarding the Graves family and their report.

"Their whole family, looking out their window, saw what appeared to be a giant string of Christmas lights in the sky. It was just hovering, and then it would move around slightly. The lights were red, green, white, and blue, this array of colors. And this thing looked to be all attached to one big object.

"Holly (the mother) calls 911 about 9:30 at night. Dispatch realized that they had a witness on the phone that was saying, 'The UFO is here, it's still here, come check it out.' The fact that they were speaking with someone who said they were currently looking at it, dispatch sent someone immediately due to the number of calls they had already received.

"Officer Jeff Velthouse is the one who reports to the scene. When he arrives, he sees the lights in the sky. He immediately takes out his binoculars. As soon as he does, he now sees a second object behind the initial string of lights. Both objects look very similar to each other. As he is watching it, one of them starts to head in his direction, moves directly overhead and starts following the path of the street he came in on. So officer Velthouse quickly gets into his vehicle to take off in pursuit of this craft, to the best of his ability. As he is in pursuit, he quickly calls into dispatch to relay what is going on."

At this point, dispatch realizes they need a little more help with what is going on in the skies over Lake Michigan, and they reach out to the local weather service, knowing they have radar capability. What follows are portions of the actual conversation between dispatch and the Weather Service of Muskegon, Michigan. The audio and transcript are readily available online.

WS: "Hello, Weather Service, Muskegon."

911: "Hi, Muskegon, this Ottawa County 911 calling."

WS: "Yah, how you doing?"

911: "Good. Do you guys have access to a radar there, don't you?"

WS: "Yes, we do."

911: "Are you getting anything weird down in the Southern Ottawa County Area?"

WS: "Anything weird? Hold on for a second."

You then hear some spoken words between two Weather Service employees that are hard to make out, and then you listen to them mention something about a tracking radar out of Chicago.

WS: "Uhm, nothing more than the usual ground flare that we get right there. Let me get a closer range."

911: "The reason I ask is because we are getting a whole bunch of calls of some strange lights in the Southern Ottawa, Northern Allegan Counties, right there near Holland City area."

WS: "Strange Lights?"

911: "Yeah, we've gotten about sixty UFO Calls."

The conversation continues for another ninety seconds, and that's when the Weather Service worker, watching the radar, sees something strange. A large object that he can't seem to follow or keep on the radar. At one point, he states he sees it around South Bend, Indiana, but then later retracts and places it back toward the Michigan Shoreline.

WS: "It's moving! It's moving toward the, ah, west, southwest. And it looks like a big blob."

The conversation continues for a while, and then:

911: "An officer in Holland City just sent me a message. I say, can you identify anything further? He says it looks like there is three to four of them."

WS: "I'm seeing three, and they are separated by, ugh, they look like a triangle. I am seeing one down by South Haven. I am seeing another one over Lake Michigan about North West of Benton Harbor and another one east of Benton Harbor, which would be near Decatur. I am seeing three of those, and they are very strong. Now I am getting another one down in Berrien County! These are huge returns! I've never seen anything like this. Not even when I am doing storms, these aren't storms. They are just popping up all over the place."

911: "This is strange. The officer says that green and red lights. Does not look like an airplane. They come together, and then they separate, and they just keep doing this all the time."

They continue to talk with one another about these objects and their path of movement for a couple more minutes. Near the end of the conversation, the Weather Service employee explains the lights are now moving over southern Lake Michigan and making their way toward Chicago. They exchange a few more words and then hang up.

After the night of March 8th, 1994, the reports of UFOs over Lake Michigan continued for quite some time. Whatever happened on that night, that had police officers and weather radar operators chasing objects in the sky, we will probably never know. To this day, the incident is considered an unsolved event.

The night of my interview with Bill Konkolesky, he graciously shared with me another incident that occurred in 1975 at Wurtsmith Air Force Base on the shores of Lake Huron. Below is Bill's account of the event.

"The night was October 30th, of 1975, but keep in mind until 1993 Wurtsmith Air Force Base housed nuclear bombers. The night in question, there were a few guards around a weapons storage area that observed this bright white light in the sky that came closer and closer until it was directly over them. As the men start to become increasingly nervous, they radio the traffic control tower, and the soldiers in the tower confirm that they are also observing this object, and have been since they caught it on radar approaching the base.

"So now we have the soldiers on the ground witnessing this object. The soldiers in the control tower see it, and it was caught on radar, all of this eliminating any chance of hallucination or illusion. Knowing they have this Unidentified Flying Object hovering above a nuclear military base, they need to get a plane up in the air and check this thing out as quickly as possible. The quickest option they have is a KC-135 Stratotanker Refueling Plane that is coming back from a run and approaching the base at the time for a landing.

"With further research into this event, I came across a published report from the Nuclear Connection Project (NCP). A part of that report is the testimony from Captain Myron Taylor, who was on the KC-135 that was ordered to pursue the UFO.

> I remember seeing lights similar to strobe lights which were flashing irregularly. We followed the lights north out over Lake Huron. Then the UFO swung south...after observing the lights, we determined that there were, in fact, two objects and the irregular flashing appeared to be some sort of signal being passed from one to the other in an effort to maintain the same position. I would estimate that our altitude was about 2,000 feet, and our speed approximately 200 knots. I would guess that we stayed close to the UFO most of the time, approximately one mile away, and each time we attempted to close on the object, it would speed away from us. We followed the UFO down to Saginaw Bay and started across the bay when we lost it because of all the fishing boat lights. On the way back [to Wurtsmith], we picked up the UFO again at our eight o'clock position. We turned away, and it proceeded to follow us. Finally, we turned back in the direction of the UFO, and it really took off back in the direction of the Bay area. I know this might sound crazy, but I would estimate that the UFO sped away from us doing approximately 1,000 knots.

"Eventually, the mysterious object left and was never seen again. Days later, the FBI, local and state police, and even the DNR were all a part of an investigation that turned up nothing! Another UFO case left unsolved. But the eeriness of that nightly visitor at Wurtsmith AFB does not stop there. In the continuation of my conversation with Bill, he finished with this:

"So, the question is, what's scarier than a UFO buzzing an Air Force base that has nuclear weapons? How about a UFO that buzzes four Air Forces bases that have nuclear weapons, within a two-week period? Wurtsmith was only one of a pattern. It started with Loring AFB in Maine on the night of October 27th, when they had a visitation from a UFO. Then on October 30th, it was the event at Wurtsmith in Michigan. Then Malmstrom AFB in Montana on the night of November 7th, a UFO was spotted, and finally, on November 9th, a UFO was spotted at Minot AFB in North Dakota. In the course of about two weeks, four nuclear-armed Air Force bases were visited by a UFO."

The list of UFO and Alien encounters around the Great Lakes region is mind-boggling. They have been going on for decades and are still reported daily. However, of all the stories, the one that is the most fascinating and sadly, the deadliest, is known as the Kinross Incident, and it happened right in my backyard.

The Kinross Air Force Base, located in the Eastern Upper Peninsula of Michigan, was built in 1943 and stayed in operation until 1977 when it was finally handed over to be used as a civilian airport. It is now the Chippewa County International Airport. The base's primary purpose was the protection of the world-famous Soo Locks, which were considered a vital piece in the war effort of WWII. During that time, it was more a refueling station. After WWII, the airport was converted to civilian use between the years 1945 and 1952. By 1952 the Cold War had begun, and so had military action in Korea, prompting the U.S. military to take back control and it became a fully functioning Air Force base.

The evening hours of the 23rd of November 1953, were a typical late fall / early winter kind of night in the U.P. of Michigan with winds mixing with snow flurries – nothing out of the ordinary. Suddenly, an Unidentified Flying Object was spotted on radar at Kinross Air Force Base over the Soo Locks. It was travelling at a speed of over 500 miles per hour heading west toward Lake Superior. Kinross AFB immediately scrambled an F-89 C Scorpion Fighter Jet, one of the best defense jets of its time, and it was flown by a seasoned pilot who was an expert on the F-89s.

The F-89 C Scorpion was a large, two-person interceptor fighter jet with close-range radar and an operator who sat behind the pilot. The two servicemen on this fateful night were the pilot, First Lt. Felix Moncla, and the radar operator, Second Lt. Robert Wilson.

The F-89 quickly scrambled and climbed to 30,000 feet to get above the clouds and hopefully obtain a better view. The issues began almost immediately when Wilson was unable to get a good hold on the object from the jet's radar system. With the help of the radar base back at Kinross, Moncla followed the calls from the base and navigated through the night sky over Lake Superior. Nearing the Keweenaw Peninsula, almost 150 miles west of the Soo Locks, where the object was first spotted, Kinross AFB radioed to Moncla and Wilson that they were nearing the object and to descend to about 8,000 feet.

As the pilots approached the UFO, radio contact between the plane and the base began to break up. The last radio contact between the two-person crew and the Kinross AFB took place around 6:52 p.m. Three minutes later, at 6:55 pm, the two blips on the radar screen became one, then the one blip disappeared.

Approximately 50 miles from the point of contact, an Air Force base in Calumet, Michigan, followed the incident and observed the craft disappear from radar. American and Canadian Air Forces and the Coast Guard immediately launched a joint search-and-rescue effort, as the incident appeared to happen over Canadian waters. The search continued night and day until winter weather forced it to end. Moncla and Wilson, and their plane, were never heard from or seen again.

The day after the Kinross Incident, when the first accounts were released, it was stated that two pilots and their plane went missing over Lake Superior in an interception mission of an Unidentified Flying Object. One of the radar operators that night was quoted as saying, "It seems incredible, but the blip just swallowed our F-89."

Like the Roswell incident, the United States Government had a different story a day later. The revised account said that the blip on the radar was a Canadian C-47 Sky Train Transport that went off course and flew into the no-fly zone over the Soo Locks. The report went on to state that pilot Moncla must have experienced some form of vertigo, which caused him to crash into Lake Superior. The problem with this story is that the Canadian military stated they had no aircraft in the area the evening of the incident.

Sadly, the press and public quickly lost interest in the incident. Then in 1955, an American Marine Corps naval aviator and writer by the name of Donald Keyhoe began to ask questions about that fateful night. Keyhoe examined some leaked documents from the incident. Far from being an open and shut case as the military claimed, they were quite confused about the incident. Keyhoe's findings brought the story back to the headlines briefly, but as before, interest quickly died out.

In 1968 wreckage of an F-89C plane washed up on the shores of Lake Superior. However, there was never a formal investigation. Why? Then, in 1999, researcher John E. L. Tenney filed a FOIA request and obtained two hundred pages of documents - far more than the fifty pages previously known to the public.

One significant item emerged from the new papers. Two of the fighter pilots who were first to approach the area the night of the incident reported an unintelligible radio transmission of Moncla talking ten minutes after the blips disappeared from radar.

The Kinross Incident made headlines again in 2006 when the Great Lakes Dive Company claimed they had sonar images of an intact jet fighter resting on the bottom of Lake Superior. This news alone would be fantastic, but the company also claimed to have sonar pictures of a "disc-shaped object" just 200 feet from the jet, embedded in the sand. Could this be the money shot everyone had been waiting for? The missing plane and a UFO together on the bottom of Lake Superior?

Alas, it was just too good to be true. Following a flurry of media attention, the website, story, and people disappeared just as quickly as the F-89 on the night of November 23, 1953.

The Kinross Incident remains unsolved to this day. No bodies, no wreckage, no clues. Only a couple of blips on the radar and the men from that night with their story. One thing is certain, however. Lt. Felix Moncla and Lt. Robert Wilson are true American heroes, giving their lives defending our nation. They were called upon to do their duty as American soldiers in the face of an unknown intruder. While doing so they made the ultimate sacrifice. To their families who still live with having no answers, our hearts go out to you. And to Moncla and Wilson, we thank you for your bravery and service.

Creatures of the Forest

Bigfoot, Wendigo, Dogman, Bearwalkers

"Never go in there alone!", he would always say when he was getting ready to tell me the stories that he knew I loved so much. As a child, hearing tales of the Gogomain Swamp, and the "monster" that lived within it, were some of the best stories my dad would share with me. He was a man of few words, but he knew how much I loved hearing about the darkness of the Swamp and what lurked within.

The Gogomain Swamp sits about an hour's drive southeast from where I grew up in Sault Ste. Marie, Michigan. It's a place where only experienced hunters and outdoorsmen dare to venture. Reported in a 1964 edition of the *Sault Ste. Marie Evening News*, the woods that make up the area are so thick that the attempts to map out the Gogomain Swamp were more difficult than mapping the Florida Everglades. In the wintertime, the Gogomain Swamp is up to thirty degrees warmer than the actual air temperature, due to the denseness of the trees. Experienced hikers and hunters have become disoriented, lost, and died before ever finding their way out.

Creepier than the swamp itself, were the tales of the monster that lived within it. Legends of the beast say that it could devour an entire full-size deer and leave nothing but the antlers and skull. The monster was also blamed for the disappearance of many experienced outdoorsmen who ventured into the swamp. With stories like this shared from one generation to another, the area eventually earned the reputation of being called "The Forest of Doom" or even more foreboding, "Michigan's Kingdom of Darkness."

As a child growing up, I was fascinated by the legends of the Gogomain Swamp and thrilled that supernatural tales like this were happening in the area where I was growing up! Any time we drove by the site, and the road that led to Gogomain, I would get chills, and my imagination would run wild about the creature that lurked just a few miles away. I wondered if it would ever come far enough out of the Swamp, and toward the main road we were on.

I went to our local library and read as much as I could on everything weird and scary around the world. I learned that the creature that lived in the Swamp was nothing more than a large predatory cat, such as a bobcat. However, the DNR had always claimed that bobcats were long gone from the Upper Peninsula of Michigan. So, how could it be a bobcat if the DNR says it is no longer there? It can't! It's a monster that lives in the Swamp. It must be! I didn't want to believe anything else.

Sadly, as technology improved and trail cams became a thing, eventually, a bobcat was caught on one within the Gogomain Swamp. Then in the early winter of 2011, a local hunter shot and killed a massive bobcat within the Swamp, weighing over forty pounds. I say "sadly" because technology finally took away one of my childhood legends and monsters. Even as an adult, writing this book, I still have a sadness that lingers when I think of the moment it happened.

However, that sadness is quickly dispelled when I start to think of the many monsters that do walk the woods of the Great Lakes Area. Stories, firsthand accounts from multiple witnesses, of creatures known as Bigfoot, Dogman, Wendigos, Shapeshifters, Deerman, The Bunnyman, and so many other names, are reported daily throughout a region that lends itself to the perfect habitat for these creatures to call home. Thick, dark, wooded areas are loaded with wildlife for food and waterways teem with fish. Offering security, food, and water, the Great Lakes region is prime for these monsters that roam among us, and in this chapter, we will explore some of those stories.

Bigfoot

You can find him on a t-shirt, ball cap, socks, probably underwear, beef jerky, social media memes, children's books, adult books, movie theaters, tv screens, cereal boxes, mugs, crossing signs, children's toys, necklaces, comic books, and bumper stickers. I even have a six-foot version of him attached to a tree in my yard, welcoming visitors to my house. It seems you can find him everywhere, yet one thing is for sure; YOU CAN'T FIND HIM, or IT, or THEM, ANYWHERE!

The creature known as Bigfoot is everywhere when it comes to pop culture these days. If you don't believe me, stop one day while you are walking through a store, any store, and look around. Chances are you will see something related to the hairy fellow. However, physical evidence that the creature, or family of creatures, known as Bigfoot, actually exists, still evades researchers across the world.

Although the name of Bigfoot dates back to only the late 1950s, the idea of a large bipedal, ape-like creature, covered in hair, and standing six to nine feet tall, has been around since the earliest days of tribes sharing stories around the fire. Every region of every country, across the globe, has its version of this creature, and they all come in different names. Bigfoot and Sasquatch are the two most famous names in the United States and Canada. Around the globe these creatures roam: Florida's Skunk Ape, the *Kushtaka* of the northwestern border with Canada, the *Sisimique* in Nicaragua, *Mapinguari* in Brazil, *Ucu* in Argentina, *Agogwe* in East Africa, *Homo Gardarensis* in Greenland, *Basajaun* in Spain, *Big Grey Man* in Scotland, *Barmanou* in Afghanistan/Pakistan, *Yeti* in Nepal/Tibet and Russia, *Kayadi* in Papua New Guinea, *Hibagon* in Japan, *Yowie* in Australia, and *Moehau* in New Zealand. And this is just scratching the surface of the different regions and names given to this creature that is living among local legends and eyewitness accounts.

The legend of "Bigfoot" began in a newspaper article published in the *Humboldt Times* in California, in 1958. The author wrote, almost in a tongue-in-cheek fashion, of a letter he received which told of loggers in the northern California woods who heard noises through the camp during the late-night hours, and found giant, non-human footprints around the grounds the next day.

What was initially thought to be a Sunday fun article for the publication soon opened a Pandora's Box. Reports of a "wild-man" through the California area had accumulated in dusty boxes in police departments across the state as well as the country. The people who had made these reports flooded the publication's office, telling of their experiences. As calls continued to come in, the author of the article quickly realized he needed to follow up with more details and further stories from the loggers. He learned that the loggers had given the name of Bigfoot to whomever, or whatever was vandalizing the camp and leaving the 16-inch tracks.

Eventually, the loggers created plaster casts of the Bigfoot tracks, and from there, the story jumped from one newspaper to another across the United States. As the story spread, so did the reports from people all over. They spoke of the large, man-like creature they had seen. Soon television picked up the creature now known as Bigfoot, and from there, the monster was thrown into a pop-culture frenzy, much like today. Dime novels and magazines soon featured Bigfoot as the primary character role.

As time went on, the fascination for Bigfoot continued to grow. However, despite the popularity of the creature through the years, one thing stands out starkly – the lack of physical proof. To date, the plaster cast footprints are the best physical evidence available. However, they are easily faked. Then there is the shaky video from phones, the hair samples that come back from analysis as inconclusive, or the fecal matter that has never come back as anything new. One piece of video evidence stands the test of time – the Patterson-Gimlin film of 1967. It was taken in the Northern California woods where the creature's name-legend was born. For kids of my time, this film was the Holy Grail of cryptids. For kids of this time, if you are unaware of this video, THANK GOD for YouTube. Please go check it out.

Despite the lack of physical evidence, one thing will always hold, and that is the eyewitness belief. Spend just five minutes with a Bigfoot witness, look in their eyes, and listen to the details of what they say they saw, or smelled, or heard, and you will soon believe in this creature!

Cases

It was early June 2015, and Julie walked to the end of her driveway to await the arrival of her daughter, Hannah, who was returning from the last day of school by bus. When I interviewed Julie, she asked for two things. One, that she and her daughter's names be changed, and two, their actual town and state never be mentioned. I promised her I would do both if she would allow me one thing, and that was to say it did happen in the Great Lakes region, and she obliged. For the sake of sharing this incident, I can say that it happened in one of the eight states that border the Great Lakes. I am sure every state that borders the Great Lakes has a story as real and detailed as this one.

Julie was a single mother, raising, in her words, her "brilliant, yet stubborn and amazing sixteen-year-old daughter." She worked two jobs to make sure that Hannah could have as normal a life as possible for a teenage girl. Hannah was finishing her sophomore year of high school, and once again ending the year with straight A's. Julie would always meet Hannah at the end of the driveway on the last day of school, and this was a tradition Hannah loved even at sixteen.

Another summer vacation was about to begin for Hannah, but this year was different. Mother and daughter were living in a new home. As soon as another Great Lakes winter ended, Julie and Hannah packed up one country home to go to another, for some new scenery. Although they had always lived in the country, this was the first time they had a farm-style house. And it seemed even more like living on a farm since it was surrounded by corn, a first for them as well.

It was a beautiful day that turned into a peaceful night. Mother and daughter were enjoying lemonade on their new covered porch. As they were chatting away, reminiscing of another school year gone by, and the excitement of moving to their new home, a sudden pungent smell came wafting through their screened-in porch. At first, they thought a skunk was visiting them, but soon the smell grew more robust and much more potent than any skunk.

Julie quickly ran to grab a flashlight to get a closer look of the yard from the safety of their closed-in porch. As they scanned the front yard, nothing seemed out of the ordinary. They turned their attention to the side of the house where the cornfield met the yard. It was then they saw something! A large, dark mass seemed to be sitting or lying on the edge of the cornfield. The flashlight's beam went across the thing on the ground, revealing a sheen of fur that covered the body. Julie realized that they were probably dealing with a wild animal. Figuring it was a bear, they decided that it was time to call it a night and head into the house.

The next morning, while Hannah was still sleeping, Julie went to get a better look at the area by the cornfield. Mostly, she wanted to make sure they did not still have an unwanted visitor. As she went outside, the pungent smell was hanging in the air but not as strong as the night before. She hoped that the animal had moved on. As she approached the area, roughly twenty yards from the house, she could see that it was gone. The cornstalks where it had lain were flattened to the ground. The damaged area was "way too big to be a bear," Julie said. "Unless it was a very restless bear and rolled around a lot during the night, or if it was a momma bear and cubs." Julie noticed within the beaten-down grass and cornstalks a trail of dried blood that led back into the cornfield. She was not about to follow that trail! Julie went on to say, "There was still the question of what was the smell? I have grown up in a family of hunters and know quite a bit about living that lifestyle and NO bear has ever given off the smell that Hannah and I experienced the night before."

Later, as they ate breakfast, Julie shared with her daughter what she had seen earlier that morning. That's when Hannah told her mother a story she had heard from the kids in her new school, shortly after they arrived at the farmhouse. The children shared with Hannah the legend of one of the owners of the old farmhouse, who lived there many decades ago – an elderly husband and wife, who kept to themselves for the most part. One day, the wife went into town and started to purchase large amounts of vegetables from the local market — more than she had ever bought before. The clerk asked her why so many vegetables, asking if they had family coming to stay with them. The elderly wife happily shared with the clerk that she was feeding a Bigfoot that had wandered on to her property. The stunned clerk listened intently. The woman went on to say that a few nights before, it showed up on their property, injured. It was lying in the cornfield, butting up against their property. It made an awful whimpering sound. The old lady, not feeling threatened or scared, believing that it was trying to ask her for help, gathered some water and food, and approached it. She laid the nourishment near the creature and went back into the house.

The next morning, she went back, and the Bigfoot was gone, but so was the food and water. However, the old lady noticed a lot of blood on the ground. Later that night it returned, and she again brought it food and water. The next morning the food and the creature were gone, and some blood remained. By now, there was no reserve in her pantry, and that's why she was at the market. Rutabagas were his favorite, according to the wife. She gathered her belongings and back to the farmhouse she went. The story spread like wildfire through the town, and of course, the locals wrote it off as a crazy old lady going mad in the old farmhouse.

The buzz continued around town for a couple of weeks, when the old lady again showed up at the local market to buy more vegetables, especially rutabagas. Everyone watched as she approached the clerk, and this time she was asked if she was still feeding the Bigfoot. She said yes, and left with her bagloads of vegetables. A month or so would go by, and finally, the wife once again arrived at the local store. But this time, she made her standard purchases that the clerk was used to seeing, and he politely asked her why she was done buying for the Bigfoot in her yard. She kindly responded that he had stopped coming around. She believed that he stayed in the cornfield during the day and went to the property line at night for food and water and continued to do this while he healed from his wound. She figured he was now strong enough and was able to get back home, wherever that was.

The following year, both the elderly husband and wife passed away. The old farmhouse would change hands many times, with no one staying for an extended period. The rumors started to grow around town that the old farmhouse was haunted, and so the legend would grow through the years.

Julie was shocked that Hannah was just now sharing this story. Hannah explained she simply did not want to scare or upset her mother. Even the kids were all laughing about it when they shared the story. However, they also asked Hannah if they had seen any ghosts or Bigfoot. Julie left the story there, not pushing the issue any farther.

Later that day, Hannah asked if she could spend the night at a friend's house. Julie was happy that her daughter was quickly finding new friends and promptly obliged. And, having a quiet night to herself sounded inviting as well. That night, as Julie sat in the living room reading a book and enjoying a cup of tea, she could not stop thinking about the incident that took place the night before and the story her daughter had shared with her earlier in the day. Julie told me how the legend of Bigfoot never really interested her, but she had heard plenty of stories of strange creatures in the woods growing up. Since she came from a family of hunters, these stories were abundant around campfires and family reunions.

Distracted by everything that had happened the night before, as well as Hannah's story, she set her book aside and walked out to the covered front porch. Immediately she was greeted with the extremely pungent smell from the night before. "I remember the feeling of my throat closing in and my stomach becoming upset," Julie said. "I don't know if the reaction was from the smell, or fear, or both. I quickly ran to grab my flashlight, and this time I grabbed my handgun as well. I was feeling happy in the fact that Hannah was gone for the night. I slowly walked to the side of the porch and pointed the light in the very same place as the night before, and there it was huddled, what looked like to be in a ball, along the side of the yard, right on the grass line of the cornfield. The smell was breathtaking, but this time I could hear, what seemed to be, labored breathing. Short and rapid breathing, over and over.

"Honestly, Tim, the ONLY thing that came to my mind was to bring it some vegetables and water! I was screaming in my head at Hannah for sharing that damn story with me," Julie said while laughing. She went back to the pantry, guessing that the creature was the same one the old farm wife cared for decades ago, and gathered some food. Sadly, she didn't have as many vegetables as she thought but gathered what she could.

Slowly she opened the door and made her way around to the side yard. Keeping the flashlight on the mass of black fur with one hand, the gun in the other, and a bunch of food pinned against her body beneath each arm, she moved closer. The labored breathing seemed to quicken as Julie approached. She quickly laid the food and water on the ground and then backed away, never taking her eyes off the nightly visitor. Once to the porch, she quickly ran in, locked the door, and went upstairs. "My bedroom is on the same side of the house as the cornfield, and I wanted to see just what this thing was. My heart was pounding, and the stench was in my nose. There was not a lot of light to see outside. The only light was coming from the living room, where I was reading my book. But, when this thing started to move, I could tell. It was HUGE and slowly made its way to the food and water. Once it had the items, it quickly went deep into the cornfield. I didn't sleep a wink that night and couldn't wait to have the sun come back up."

Before Hannah came home that day, Julie was outside at the break of dawn. Once again, she could see where this creature bedded down, and still, she could see what looked like dried blood. Then Julie noticed something new, the footprint! The night before she had not put the food and water right by the creature, she was too frightened. She figured she had put the food about six feet, or more, away. Earlier that day, they had a decent rainfall, causing the ground to be wet, and in that damp ground, now left the signs all Bigfoot hunters want to find. "I measured it myself from heel to the tip of the big toe, and it measured no less than twenty inches!"

"Hannah is now married, with family, and does not even live in the United States. She has never seen another Bigfoot but knows all too well of their existence. This is a secret we promised we would always keep. I now live alone in this beautiful old farmhouse. We do not want our lives, or its life, ruined by media, thrill-seekers or Hollywood. Our Bigfoot still comes around to this day. At least, now, it's not just when there is an injury. I will always know he is there, by the smell, or the sound he will make, to let me know. He doesn't come around often, but when he does, I always make sure I have the vegetables ready, especially the rutabaga.

"I don't have a clue what or who it is. I don't know if it's a male or female, I just refer to it as a male. I don't want to know, and I don't need to know anything more. There is something pretty special about this property, and I love being a part of it. I do believe he is out there, watching over the land, the farmhouse, and me. Oh, and just for the record, this farmhouse is NOT haunted. I believe it was the Bigfoot that was scaring everyone away. But when it's an old house on a piece of property, it MUST be a ghost, not a Bigfoot," Julie laughed.

This story was never about fame or recognition for Julie. She never, nor will she ever, go looking for more publication on this story. Sometimes it's just enough to know someone, who knows someone, who knows someone, and happens to have their email!

This account of Bigfoot tells the story of a kind creature. Most Bigfoot stories never are about attacks or extremely negative experiences. Most people tell of logs or large boulders thrown in their direction in self-defense, trying to scare them away. Some cryptozoologists even think that the foul smell most accompanied in a Bigfoot event, is also a form of self-defense, much like the skunk. Through the years and all the reports, it seems Bigfoot simply wants to continue to live among us but will scare us to defend itself. However, can we be so sure that the other monsters who live within our Northern Woods are as willing to cohabitate?

Bearwalkers

Could it be that reports of Bigfoot are nothing more than sightings of bears standing on their hind legs? Some Bigfoot skeptics often hang their hat on this theory. Believers, however, will kindly remind the nay-sayers that a bear on its hind haunches still does not equal Bigfoot's stature.

What if the bear is not truly a bear, but a shapeshifting being, assuming the guise of a larger-than-average bear? This could be the case if the sighting is of a Bearwalker!

A Native American legend, still strongly believed today, is of the "Mockwamosa", the Bearwalker cult. To be a member of this cult is not something to be desired, if you wish to live a good and wholesome life. Those who possess the power are often described as sitting in church on Sunday and doing the Devil's work on Monday. Bearwalkers are shapeshifters that can take the shape of any animal they wish. However, the bear is the most frequently chosen form. Those who possess the power of the Bearwalker must use the ability to take at least one human life a year, or the very power they possess will be turned against them.

The possessed, once in bear form, walk upright and are surrounded by lights as they hunt and stalk their next victim. Many witnesses claim to see great lights, or even fireballs, deep within the woods. By these signs they know that there is a Bearwalker nearby.

When the Bearwalker is near death, they must pass their power, or curse, to another human. The process is simple. They call an innocent over to them and tell them that they have something for them. Then the Bearwalker reveals itself to the victim and the power is transferred. Once passed on, there is no going back and a new Bearwalker is born.

Is a shapeshifting Bearwalker the same creature we call Bigfoot? Probably not, and I will gladly file Bearwalker into its own category and add to the stacks of files containing these wonderful and amazing creatures.

Dogman

Much like Bigfoot, Dogman also stands quite tall and covered in hair or fur. Many eyewitnesses estimate its height is six feet or more. The big difference between them is their stature. Where Bigfoot is said to be thick and broad, Dogman stands with a slenderer build.

Growing up in the Upper Peninsula of Michigan, stories of Bigfoot were everywhere, but Dogman came later in our years. We often say, when presenting and speaking across the region, if we had heard and known about Dogman growing up, I don't think we would have been running through the

Northern Woods. There is something about the Dogman that just creeps the heck out of me!

Although stories of the Dogman are all around the world, just as they are for Bigfoot, the Great Lakes region can lay claim to the most popular. Some of the more famous Dogman claims come from Wisconsin where it is known as the Beast of Bray Road. This Dogman was made famous by a well-known author and friend of ours, Linda Godfrey.

Early in Linda's career, she wrote for a now-defunct publication known as the *Walworth County Week*, or as Linda refers to it, "The Week." Being close to Christmas, it was a particularly slow news cycle, and as any good journalist does, Linda was searching high and low for an exciting story to help fill the pages. She was the new kid at the paper and was hungry for a story. She had heard reports of a sizeable dog-like animal in an area known as Bray Road, in Elkhorn, Wisconsin. Linda had found her story, and her editor was happy to let her follow some leads.

One of the first townspeople Linda interviewed shared with her the experience she had late one night on Bray Road, coming home from work. Lorianne Endrizzi was driving down the long, dark country road when she noticed a canine creature off to the side. She said the animal was not standing there on four legs but rather knelt on knees as a human would be, and in its paws, it held roadkill. Endrizzi later told Linda she was sure the animal was Satanic. It was Enrizzi's description of the creature kneeling at the side of the road that Linda drew from, and used in the forthcoming article. This hand-drawn sketch is now famous worldwide in the cryptozoological world.

Another witness to the Beast of Bray Road shared with Linda an even more frightening tale. One night she was driving down Bray Road when she was sure she ran over an animal. Worried she might have hit a dog, she immediately stopped the car and got out to check. That's when an animal she had never seen before came bounding out of the long grass on the side of the road and ran toward her! She stated how it ran on two legs and had the shape and head of a dog. She remembers vividly the sound the feet made as it ran up the road. It was the sound a human would make when running hard. She quickly jumped in her car and sped off as soon as she could, watching this beast trail behind her until it took one last leap at the vehicle, leaving claw marks on the back hood.

Story after story, eyewitness after eyewitness, filled Linda's notepad, to the point where she was ready to write her story, and on December 31, 1991, the original article of "The Beast of Bray Road" was released. By January of 1992, the report had spread like wildfire across the country, and Linda Godfrey's life and career would never be the same. Nor would Elkhorn, Wisconsin.

Today, Linda is one of the leading authorities on Dogman, Man-Dog, and Werewolves. She has dedicated her life to researching, writing, and speaking on these subjects. Thanks to the power of Linda's pen, Wisconsin was put on the map as a hotspot for Dogman. But one state actually lays claim to the beast, by name, and that's my home state of Michigan and The Michigan Dogman.

Michigan is a fantastic place to grow up and grow old. Surrounded by all but one of the Great Lakes, and the home where Social Distancing was born, in the Upper Peninsula, the state is the perfect hiding place for any creature! After all, if our "normal wolves" can be over seven feet in length, what other creatures could be hiding in the Michigan woods?

In the Vol. 12 No. 8, 2020 edition of the *Great Lakes Pilot*, the front-page story presents the account of a Michigan hunter, Earl Eastman. Eastman tells of the day in November 1935, when he and his buddies were in the third day of deer hunting in Northern Michigan. But it wouldn't be a famous Michigan Whitetail they came home with that day, but rather a mammoth timber wolf, measuring 7 feet, 11 inches long. It stood 39 inches at the shoulders and 12-3/4 inches across the skull. Accompanying the article is a picture of this giant wolf, and it is a sight to see.

What was born out of a radio bit for a morning radio show in the late 1980s, quickly blew up into a legend all its own. However, the idea of a Man-Dog-like creature roaming the woods was being shared among the Native American tribes, known as the Waheela, for generations. *Radio Morning Show* producer, Steve Cook, on WTCM out of Traverse City, Michigan, was preparing for his April first (Fools) show in 1987. Using his interest in legends and lore of the area, Steve created a song known as "The Legend," which told the story of a dog-like beast that appeared in the 7th year of every decade, terrorizing all those who came in contact with it.

Openly, Cook admits in a 2011 *Detroit Free Press* article, that he knew nothing of the Michigan Dogman when he created this song, but rather, made the creature within his song based on many stories and legends. After playing his song that morning on the radio, Cook soon found out that the very animal in his song seemingly lived in the Northern Michigan woods. The phones to the studio and office started ringing immediately, with listeners of the morning show sharing stories handed down to them from parents and grandparents, and even firsthand accounts that happened to the callers.

Just as the name Bigfoot was a relatively new name given to an ancient creature, it seems the same happened for The Michigan Dogman. More and more stories started to appear, and people came forward to share their stories of a creature that seemed to first appear as a large black dog. As witnesses approached it, that's when it would rear up on its hind legs, showing it was not just a quadrupedal, but also a bipedal creature. Witnesses say it stands over six feet tall, has hypnotizing blue eyes, and lets out a howl and scream better than anything Hollywood could produce.

The earliest reported story of The Michigan Dogman seems to originate from Wexford County, Michigan, in 1887. Two lumberjacks were working in an area when they started to notice large dog-like prints in the morning. Horses began to disappear overnight and eventually the creature made itself known to the lumberjacks. What they saw, and reported, was a large creature on two legs, standing over seven feet tall with the head of a dog but the body of a human.

Another story from the late 1930s tells of a hunter in Paris, Michigan, who reported five wolves attacked him in the woods, just around dusk, but one of them walked around on two legs!

There are countless stories and accounts of run-ins with the Dogman, and even a nice collection of supposed photos can be found. However, one piece of video continues to be the talk of the cryptid chapter of Dogman. It is called the Gable Film. In 2007 a grainy piece of tape appeared, which was said to have been found on 8mm film from the 1970s. It shows family videos that run almost six minutes long, with no volume. Near the end of the film, the camera holder focuses on something crouched down, off in the distance. Seconds later, this thing stands up and runs toward the camera. The person holding the camera then takes off running, the camera still in hand but now pointing to the ground. Soon the camera drops, and the last thing the viewer sees is what appears to be the mouth and fangs of the creature.

For a moment in time, this film was believed to be to The Michigan Dogman what the Patterson-Gimlin film was to Bigfoot. However, colossal doubt was cast on the film when the TV show, *Monster Quest*, claimed to have debunked its authenticity. But still, diehard believers hold on to their truth of what can be seen in the film.

Another piece of evidence that the hardcore believers hold on to is the 2006 OnStar incident. On the night of January 6, in Troy, Michigan, a husband and wife were driving down a country road when a large animal suddenly ran in front of them. They swerved to miss the animal and crashed upside down in a ditch. They activated OnStar.

In the call, you hear one of the passengers talking to Kyle, the OnStar operator. They explain what happened and that neither of them is hurt badly but they need assistance. Kyle tells them to hold while he contacts emergency services. When Kyle comes back, he informs them that emergency services are on the way, then begins to converse with the occupants of the vehicle. This is standard protocol to calm the people in the situation. Kyle asks what ran in front of them, and the guy responds, "I don't know what the hell it was, but it was big. It looked like a great big dog…but it was standing up." Then Kyle responds, "Was it a bear?" The guy replies, "Maybe, I'd…" Then you hear the growl of some creature, the screams of the people within the vehicle, and then the call drops. A second or two of silence, and then Kyle says, "Sir? Hello? Are you still there? Sir?"

Stories of Dogmen are all over the state and the Great Lakes region. It may be that the area's plentiful fresh food and water attract the creatures. Sightings are most prevalent along the shores of the Great Lakes – which offer abundant hunting, fishing and shelter. No matter which state version of this creature you may see, let's just say this is not one you want to pet.

Man's best friend? I don't think so!

Wendigo

This creature may be the least well-known of the three wooded monsters we are sharing in this chapter. However, it may be the most known to the Native Americans in the Great Lakes region.

Wendigo, or Windigo, to some, means the same thing. However, others say there is a distinct difference between the two. Wendigo is the physical representation of the man-beast in the Northern Woods, while Windigo is the man-eating spirit that haunts the Northern Woods. But, for the sake of this book, Wendigo will represent both.

The Wendigo is a forest creature that has been around since the First Nations Algonquian. It is known throughout the Great Lakes region and farther north into Canada and Nova Scotia. It is a creature that is a harbinger of bad news, and that bad news is, if you see it, you're toast. It's a creature that feeds on the flesh of men. It also can possess a person and make them do terrible things. It is even believed that a Wendigo was once a human who was transformed by eating the flesh of other people.

Through the different regions, the Wendigo description changes a bit but most of the characteristics stay the same. The creature possesses dirty fangs or claws, has a long tongue, glowing eyes, yellowish skin, and a body covered in matted hair. It is described as a fantastic hunter – its victims never have a chance. It is exceptionally gaunt and has an insatiable appetite. One of the best tools the Wendigo has for hunting, and possibly the creepiest, is the ability to mimic a human voice. They often lure their victims with the sounds of someone needing help.

Sightings of the Wendigo are much less common in modern times than Bigfoot or Dogman. The believers in Wendigo will gladly remind you that to see Bigfoot or Dogman is to see a fantastic creation of Nature. There are no witnesses to the Wendigo, because to see it is to see the Devil himself, and you will not live to talk about it.

With all these fantastic stories of creatures roaming our Great Lakes woods, the question remains, why do we still not have a body for any of them? There are a few theories. The oldest is simply that these creatures are evolved and smart enough to last all these years, so they are smart enough to bury or hide their own. Two other theories have been advanced in more recent years. One is that they are interdimensional creatures. According to this theory, there are places on this planet that are portals which open and allow creatures, and even beings to travel between different worlds. The last theory is that these types of creatures are hitching rides from ET and coming down in UFOs.

Although I love all ideas of what could allow these monsters to walk among us, I tend to stick to the good old-fashioned belief that they do live among us and take care of their own when needed. No matter your faith in their existence, please remember this. Next time you are walking in the beautiful woods and forests of the Great Lakes, and you hear the snap of something behind you, don't look back, think happy thoughts, and leave.

Little People of the Lakes

Imps, Fairies, Gnomes, Will-o'-the-wisps

"WE SAW A LEPRECHAUN IN OUR YARD."

I could see the woman was immediately scrutinizing my reaction, searching my face for any sign of disbelief. "Really?" I replied. "Tell me all about it."

I had been investigating a waterfront area on Mackinac Island, Michigan, one October night, leading a group of people who were vacationing on the island that weekend as part of a paranormal event. It was cold, windy, and damp, and although I'd grown up in the north, I had failed to pack appropriately for the quickly changing autumn weather. I was concluding my session with the current group, who would then move on to an indoor location, someplace with heat and a roof, while I would continue to monitor the rocky shoreline, and endure the rapidly deteriorating conditions.

As the ghost hunters congregated and began packing their tools (cameras, audio recorders, electromagnetic field detectors, and any of the latest gadgets used on the current slew of paranormal reality shows in order to seek out the unknown), a middle-aged couple approached me with the usual paranormal small talk: how long had I been investigating, where was my favorite haunted

45

location, and what was the scariest thing I'd seen. Then, they related the tale of the leprechaun.

The woman continued with her story: "We were at our vacation property a few hours south of here, near the shore of Lake Michigan. As we were walking through a heavily wooded area, we both noticed something shuffling near the edge of the forest. It looked like a small man dressed in dark clothes, easily shorter than three feet, with a ruddy complexion. He stopped and looked at us for a couple seconds but took off into the forest as soon as my husband took his picture."

"Wait a minute," I interjected. "You have an actual picture of him?"

"Sure," she casually replied. "I keep it in an old storage chest at home. I haven't taken it out in years, because it still creeps me out. We've been back to the property dozens of times since then, and even though it's been a few years since we saw him, I'm still nervous when I walk in those woods alone."

As the groups began to rotate, I hurriedly gave the couple my contact information and pleaded with them to send me an email or copy of the photo. While they hiked up the slick, muddy walkway, they assured me they would dig it out as soon as they returned home and forward me the image. They didn't.

Had they encountered this "leprechaun" as their story went, or were they merely trying to see how gullible I could be when it came to such things? As strange as it may sound to the average person, encounters with "little people" (leprechauns, gnomes, elves, fairy folk) are not as uncommon as they may think. According to *The Steiger Questionnaire of Mystical, Paranormal, and UFO Experiences*, a survey designed by paranormal researchers and authors Brad and Sherry Steiger, 29% of the more than 30,000 people surveyed claimed to have had an encounter with elves, fairies, or some type of nature spirit.

The mere mention of fairies and leprechauns calls to mind pop culture versions of the mystical beings – for example, characters from Disney cartoons and spokes-creatures for breakfast cereal. However, legends of the little people and nature spirits appear in nearly all cultures. These stories share many similarities and are often much darker than their popular, modern representations.

When we look back to the history of the Great Lakes region, we find Native American legends ripe with tales of these creatures, along with multiple interpretations of their origins. One such story, the Ojibwe legend of Wa-Dais-Ais-Imid (He of the Little Shell), relates the tale of a young brave who stops growing while still an infant. Little Shell becomes a trickster and develops the power of invisibility, allowing him to carry out his shenanigans undetected by the fully grown members of his tribe. When the time comes for him to leave his people, Little Shell goes to live amongst the mountains and rocks, areas where the waters are clean and the air is pure. These are the areas where one is most likely to catch a glimpse of Wa-Dais-Ais-Imid and his peers, the Puck-Wudj-Ininees, or Vanishing Little People.

Another legend adapted specifically to the northern lakes region is that of the maiden O-We-Nee, the beautiful daughter of a powerful chief. O-We-Nee marries the son of The Evening Star, who transports her and her family to his lodge in the sky where they live as ethereal beings. The couple has a son who, upon hearing tales of his earthbound tribesmen, wants more than anything to be a brave hunter. When he is old enough to properly use a bow, he draws an arrow and takes aim at one of the birds of the lodge, which turns out to be a sister of O-We-Nee, who in death reverts back to her human form. With the spilling of innocent blood, Evening Star banishes the family back to earth, but in the diminutive size of the Puck-Wudj-Ininees, to live out their days on an island sacred to the Ojibwe people, Mich-il-i-mack-in-aw, nowadays, simply Mackinac. On summer nights, any person brave enough to venture to the rocky shore of the island is said to run the risk of encountering their lights shooting along the coast, which the natives would come to refer to as the Mish-In-E-Mok-In-Ok-Ong, the Dancing Turtle Spirits.

These "dancing lights" are still reported by residents and visitors to Mackinac today. On a group investigation of the Island's coast (not the same night as the leprechaun story, but in similar conditions), I spotted rapidly moving figures of light shooting along the shoreline. Although many who hear of the phenomena attempt to explain away these frequently spotted lights as fireflies, my firsthand encounter with the puckwudgies convinced me that bugs had nothing to do with what was being observed. As we continued to watch the "fairy lights," as most islanders refer to them, we noticed that they seemed to come closer to our group, as if feeling us out. Although they didn't openly reply to our attempts to communicate, after a few minutes it was clear they had no fear of humans. Two of the lights shot past one of the women in the group. As she recorded the phenomena on her phone, another five of these lights, all bright white, flew up to her leg and one after the other, rapidly changed course, so as not to make contact. Even so, they came within mere inches before zipping around her!

So, what exactly are these "fairies," and what is their true origin? In Rosemary Ellen Guiley's *Encyclopedia of Ghosts and Spirits*, fairies are defined as "a type of supernatural being, neither ghost, god, nor demi-god, which exists on earth and either helps or harms humankind. Fairy beliefs are universal and are strikingly similar." She goes on to explain that "fairies are given various names and descriptions, but in almost all cases are diminutive, even tiny. They may be beautiful or ugly, may resemble humans, or have wings and carry wands or pipes. They usually are invisible save to those with clairvoyant sight; they can make themselves visible to humans if they so desire." Although this description may have similarities to the traditional legends of the Puk-wudj-i-nees, or Pukwudjies, it seems a bit off from the sentient lights that we encountered that night.

Although a plethora of these tales of dancing lights have been recorded on Mackinac over the centuries, the fairies don't restrict themselves to the island. In 1721, a voyageur travelling to Fort Michilimackinac, located at the current day Mackinaw City, Michigan, told of traveling through the woods south of the fort near dusk when he found himself flanked by small white lights, which flittered through the foliage on either side of the trail. Although normally silent, aside from the sounds of nature, the woods seemed to come alive with the pitch of light laughter, seemingly emanating from the lights as they followed him along the darkening trail. The French traders had their own name for these beings: *Les Dames Blanches*, the White Ladies, believed in French folklore to be a form of female nature spirit, and voyageurs around the lakes told many tales of similar encounters.

Other sightings, such as the leprechaun encounter, are distinctly different enough from the fairy forms to fall into a category of their own, yet all seem to fit into the realm of nature spirits rather than cryptid beings.

Gnomes

Another figure that could be grouped with the leprechaun is the gnome. Not long ago, I was interviewing a client for a potential haunting investigation. When asked for descriptions of the activity, the owner rattled off a list of purported occurrences: lights turning on, disembodied voices, objects being moved, and the occasional appearance of an evil gnome. Of the encountered phenomena, three are reported often; the gnome, however, was a first for me!

"My sister is the only one who's had experiences with the gnome," the client said. "She describes it as the epitome of evil! Just the vibe it gave off was enough to make her run out of the house."

Although we didn't encounter the creature during our team's investigation of the property, I've come across too many reports of the diminutive, human-looking beings throughout the Great Lakes region to completely discount these run-ins as overactive imaginations at work.

Some of the best gnome encounters may be those reported in the northwestern region of Lake Michigan, near the Wisconsin coastline. The Devil's Punchbowl, located four miles outside of Menominee, is a natural wilderness formation carved out by the last glacial period. The heavily vegetated area is popular among hikers and bird watchers and may also be home to at least one family of little folk. Visitors to the Punchbowl have reported various strange phenomena, including the sighting of a small man, roughly two-feet tall with a long white beard, running up the side of a rock outcropping and disappearing into a tunnel. Legends have long held that the area is a place of great natural energies, making it an ideal habitat for a family of nature spirits.

Farther south in the Dairy State, more sightings of the wee ones have been reported. Outside Milwaukee, a young woman was taking an afternoon stroll in a wooded area near her home when she heard what she described as a faint voice, like the sound of a radio with the volume turned nearly all the way down. As she turned in the direction of the sound, she was startled to find a small, elf-like figure relaxing on a tree trunk. The woman claimed to have had a brief interaction with the little man who, after their encounter, disappeared without a trace. Similar reports have been made in lakeside communities surrounding southern Lake Michigan, including villages in Illinois and Indiana.

A unique sighting of multiple gnomes gathered in a group occurred in the 1950s in Dearborn, Michigan, where a resident claimed to witness no less than 15 men wearing dark green "elf suits," pointed hats included! His description noted the men as taller than would normally be expected of a gnome/elf-type creature, yet not appearing to be quite human. To further complicate the matter, the sighting of a nearby "craft," complete with flashing, multi-colored lights, was reported in the same area. The gnome's large size and the presence of the strange vehicle may tilt this encounter more toward the realm of an extraterrestrial visitation than an elf sighting. Might all these sightings be of extraterrestrial or possibly interdimensional origin?

The Nain Rouge

Although most claims declare run-ins with little folk as singular events, one figure has appeared on multiple occasions for centuries, and it would seem with a specific purpose. The dreaded *Nain Rouge*, or Red Dwarf of Detroit, is said to have been spotted on nights before nearly all major disasters striking the city, an ominous omen of evil tidings for Motown.

Some of the more famous Nain sightings include:

- In July of 1763, the Nain was spotted running along the beach by members of a doomed British garrison on the night prior to the Battle of Bloody Run, when troops from Fort Detroit attempted a failed surprise attack on Chief Pontiac's camp, ending with the forewarned warriors killing and wounding many of the soldiers.

- When the Great Detroit Fire decimated the city in 1805, a number of the habitants claimed to see the dwarf running through the burning structures.

- During the unrest that ultimately led to the Detroit Riots of 1967, stories of the Nain Rouge being spotted on rooftops in the inner city spread through the area.

- In March of 1976, two utility workers claimed to see a small figure climbing an electric pole, then jumping better than twenty feet to the ground and running off. The following day, one of the worst blizzards in the city's history hit Detroit, stranding thousands of people and knocking out power to a large portion of the area.

This red-faced creature seems to pop up prior to every major disaster to plague the Motor City, but how far back does the tale of the Red Dwarf reach? According to one of the most detailed, and the oldest written accounts I was able to uncover, the origin of the Nain Rouge's tenure in Detroit goes back to the very founding of the first settlement.

In her book *Legends of Le Detroit*, published in 1883 by Marie Caroline Watson Hamlin, the coming of the Nain Rouge was first foretold in 1701. In that year, the governor of New France held a party in Quebec to honor Antoine de la Mothe Cadillac, who had recently returned from Europe. France's Colonial Minister had bestowed upon Cadillac the commission of Commandant and a land grant along what would become known as the Detroit River. Cadillac had orders to establish a French fort and colony. The new settlement was meant to serve as a center for French interests in the bustling fur trade and close an important supply route to the hated British who were also actively establishing colonies and directing commerce in this region.

During the height of the evening's revelry, a strange old woman wandered into the room, capturing the attention of all. Described as being unusually tall with a dark complexion and glittering eyes, and dressed in eccentric garments, she introduced herself as Mere Minique, *La Sorcière*, and she had come to discern the fortune of any inquisitive enough to extend her their palm (and a few coins).

Though the more superstitious among the crowd shied away, many of the partygoers found her to be a delightful addition to the gathering and lined up to have their fortunes told. Once she had worked her way to Cadillac, she glared with a foreboding air. "*Sieur*," she said, "yours is a strange destiny. A dangerous journey you will soon undertake. You will found a great city which one day will have more inhabitants than New France now possesses, and many children will nestle around your fireside."

After a pause, Cadillac commanded that she continue, wishing to hear more of this great metropolis he was destined to establish. Mere Minique complied, warning of a dire future to come, including great bloodshed from skirmishes with the Indians and British, and that his eventual death would occur in France, with his children inheriting nothing from his great ventures. This would all happen should he follow the wrong path. The soothsayer left him with a final warning: "Appease the Nain Rouge. Beware of offending him." The prophecy frightened Cadillac's wife; however, Antoine himself was unmoved, brushing it off as nothing more than a simple parlor game by an exotic old woman.

The following day, Cadillac assembled his group of soldiers, craftsmen, and voyageurs and set out on the long southern journey to his future home.

It would be late July before the expedition reached its destination. After exploring and surveying the areas along the riverfront, the best tactical location was agreed upon and the land plotted for construction of the new fort.

Upon completion, Cadillac christened the new outpost Fort Pontchartrain, after the colonial minister who had granted him both title and land. Soon afterwards, settlers constructed a church, barracks, and log homes nearby, establishing the foundation for what would eventually grow into the city of Detroit.

Years passed, and the community continued to grow and flourish, as did Antoine Cadillac's wealth and stature within the colony. However, not all who settled in this outpost on the river found prosperity. On their way home from a social gathering one evening, the Cadillacs overheard a conversation between a few of the less fortunate newcomers to the settlement, who complained of the Cadillac's arrogance and privilege as others lived in squalor. As the couple hurried by, wishing to avoid an altercation, Mrs. Cadillac heard one of the men claim that his wife had recently encountered *le petit homme rouge* (the little red man), and that ruin was surely on the way for the founding family.

Much as at their farewell party in Quebec years before, when Mere Minique had first made her dire prediction, Antoine ignored his wife's concern and scoffed at the claim the habitant had made regarding the Red Dwarf. The couple briskly continued their short distance home.

As the Cadillacs neared their property, they were startled by the abrupt appearance of a diminutive figure trotting along the beachfront in their direction. As the little man crossed into the moonlit path, they were able to get a better look at him. Indeed, to Mrs. Cadillac's horror, he appeared to be a dwarf, with bright, glistening eyes and a deep red complexion. But what may have been most disturbing to the couple was the mouth full of sharp, pointy teeth which he flashed in a malevolent grin.

Rather than heed the warning of the old fortune teller, the short-tempered Antoine lashed out at the figure with his cane, yelling, "Get out of my way, you red imp!" As the cane flew in the dwarf's direction, there erupted an evil, mocking laugh from the creature as he vanished into the night. The Cadillacs hurriedly rushed inside their home, Antoine barricading the door as his wife wept and carried on that his actions would surely bring ruin to the family. Although he continued to scoff at the notion, he became a bit more apprehensive of what his actions may have set in motion.

Soon after the harrowing encounter, Cadillac was summoned back to Montreal, where he was promptly arrested and confined. It seemed not everyone was happy with his past dealings, through which he had acquired his position and lands. His old enemies had spent years conspiring against him. Although these charges (whatever they may have been are not mentioned in any version of the tale I've come upon) did not stick, Antoine was forced to sell most of his holdings in order to pay for an expensive trial, after which his superiors reassigned him. He had to leave his beloved settlement at Detroit and relocate to the Deep South to oversee French holdings in Louisiana. He eventually returned to France, where he spent his final days, passing away with no property and little money to leave to his children, much as Mere Minique had prophesized many years before.

Had Cadillac heeded the warning and offered the Nain Rouge a friendly hand rather than a swat with his cane, might things have turned out differently? For that matter, is there ever the chance to avert destiny once the Nain is encountered? Is his appearance a harbinger of doom, with no option of an alternate outcome?

Nowadays Detroit's *Marche du Nain Rouge*, held on the Sunday following the first day of spring, has grown into an annual festival featuring a parade along with performances by regional artists and entertainers, and naturally an appearance by the Nain himself, or at least a costumed human geared up to play the part. Depending upon which reveler you encounter, the celebration is either held to appease the Red Dwarf, as Antoine Cadillac was forewarned to do back at the city's founding, or to banish him for another year, freeing the people of Detroit from his threats. Either way, the Nain Rouge has ingrained himself in the lore of the Motor City, and as Marie Hamlin stated in her long ago published tale: "…should misfortune ever threaten the bonnie City of the Straits, the Nain Rouge will again appear to give the signal of warning."

Fairies, gnomes, leprechauns, dwarfs…all labels associated with nature spirits, and so much more. Do the energies of the Great Lakes lend themselves to attract such creatures? Although they run the gamut from benevolent to malicious in various stories, many of the encounters seem to indicate these beings are simply living alongside humanity, possibly in an overlapping dimension, with little interest in human activity. For those who encounter these little folks, the impact on their lives tends to be anything but small.

Airborne Anomalies

THE LAND AND SEAS OF THE GREAT LAKES REGION HIDE STRANGE CREATURES APLENTY. Enthusiasts organize searches of the forests and lakes for these cryptids, based on scant eyewitness reports and the occasional controversial photograph. But what about the skies above? Looking back to pre-European days, the lore of native tribes is rich with tales of fearsome birds and strange winged creatures soaring over their encampments and hunting grounds, threatening to make a meal of the young brave unlucky enough to end up in their talons. Considering modern reports of flying cryptids inhabiting the skies above, the line between truth and legend may be blurrier than assumed.

Thunderbirds

The prime airborne entity in Native American and Canadian mythology is the Thunderbird. Legend holds this giant feathered beast was so large that the flapping of its wings could create thunder and it had the ability to shoot lightning bolts from its eyes. Like the *Roc* of Arabian lore, which was said to be powerful enough to fly off with a grown elephant, the Thunderbird would snatch up large animals including moose, wolves, and tribe members unfortunate enough to cross its path.

During his 1673 journey through the Great Lakes region, Jesuit priest Jacques Marquette was warned to watch the skies above his canoe for the *Piasa*, an Illini Indian version of the Thunderbird. Marquette described in his diary large cliff paintings of the bird that was said to boast a 50-foot wingspan and have talons large enough to spear a full- grown deer. Though these creatures have been written off as tribal legends, is it possible that a race of giant birds may have existed in prehistoric North America, and could there still be lingering descendants roaming the skies?

In the 1890s, a newspaper in Benton Harbor, Michigan, reported the appearance of a gigantic bird with dark speckled feathers. According to the story, the creature was terrorizing local farmers, who claimed the bird was an omen of poor weather and bad luck to come. The paper went so far as to blame the bird's enormous wings for causing a water vortex to form in Lake Michigan that allegedly sank the steam ship *Chicora* in 1895. Whether the articles were based on factual sightings, or were sensationalized accounts to sell papers, the local population found themselves looking up in the sky that summer, wary of ending up a meal in some giant nest.

In April 1948 a rash of giant bird sightings plagued the state of Illinois. Early in the month, an officer at a U.S. military installation near Alton reported spotting a monstrous bird, which he believed to be larger than a standard military aircraft, circling the area. The following week, a couple near Caledonia told authorities that a similar bird was flying over their farmland; a creature large enough to make them fear for the safety of their livestock. They had mistaken the bird for a small airplane, until it began flapping its wings. That same week, a trucker in Freeport reported the monster, and a 12-year-old boy in Glendale swore to his parents he'd spotted a bird as big as an airplane flying over their neighborhood. Other sightings were reported through the spring as news outlets began pushing the story to the public. By summer, the great bird had either moved on or had gone into hiding, but it would not be the last time the land of Lincoln was terrorized by such a creature.

Almost 30 years later, a mother in Lawndale, Illinois, was in for the fright of her life when she experienced a first-hand encounter with a pair of possible Thunderbirds. It was a hot July day in 1977. Ruth Lowe stood at the window, watching her ten-year-old son Marlon playing in the back yard when she noticed the child standing frozen in place as a large shadow passed overhead. Suddenly, Marlon began to run toward the house, letting out a panicked scream. Ruth ran outside just in time to see a giant, black bird with a white-ringed neck swoop out of the sky and snatch the child in mid-run. Terrified, she pursued the creature that was attempting to fly off with her son, who had been carried 30 feet across the yard by the enormous beast. Her panicked chase paid off as the bird dropped the boy before ascending. The already horrified mother was in for a greater shock, as she witnessed a second bird of a similar size join the monster as it flew back into the atmosphere. As incredible as this encounter sounds, several of the Lowes' neighbors witnessed it. This incident was just the beginning of a flap of giant bird sightings that would plague Illinois once again, as random sightings of a huge airborne creature were reported throughout that summer.

Farther north, just east of the Minnesota border with northern Wisconsin, another oversized avian dominated the skies. In June 2005, John Bolduan was enjoying a vacation at a rural cabin in the Webb Lake wilderness area. Taking advantage of the sunshine and warm weather, John headed out on his bike for some fresh air and exercise, pedaling off to explore one of the nature trails surrounding the lake.

When he came upon a clearing, John was surprised to see what he thought was an emu standing in the middle of the field. He stopped to get a better look at the bird. He estimated it stood between seven and eight feet tall and was roughly six feet in length, with dark grey feathers. Not wanting to startle the bird, he hid his bike at the edge of the field, then crouched down in the high grass and quietly attempted to approach it. As he got within yards of the bird, it caught a glimpse of him and took flight, exposing what John believed to be a 20-foot wingspan, many times larger than any bird known to inhabit the area.

Similarly, a fisherman in Lake Huron had a close encounter with what he believed to be a Thunderbird, or at least a bird much larger than anything thought to exist today. It was June of 2012 when Mark and his father were out for a sunny day on the lake. As they trolled near the village of Spanish, Ontario, located on the far north shore of Huron, Mark noticed a large, moving shadow covering the boat. Gazing up, they were shocked to see what Mark described as something many times larger than a bald eagle, with a wingspan so immense it blocked out the sun. A similar creature had been reported the prior year flying over a nearby upper Michigan forest, lending credence to the theory there may be a family of these rare beasts nesting in the remote woodlands of northern Michigan and Ontario.

These giant birds are by no means "normal" animals. With over 130 different species native to the region, it's not too difficult to believe an oddly oversized avian or possibly a very rare creature on the brink of extinction may have descendants still gliding through the skies.

Not all flying creature encounters resemble ancient birds or other known species. Tales of the Mothman, a large flying cryptid described as being neckless, with glowing red eyes and large wings, are most commonly associated with northern West Virginia where a rash of sightings of the cryptid began in 1966 in and around the town of Point Pleasant. The creature is believed to have been an omen of the Silver Bridge collapse in 1967. In December, at the height of the Christmas shopping season, 46 people died when the bridge fell into the Ohio river.

Although commonly assumed to be one solitary creature, could there actually be *Mothmen*? Sightings around the Great Lakes have led to just such a conclusion.

In the summer of 2008, a carload of picnickers were driving down a rural road outside of Pellston, Michigan, when a creature very like the Mothman swooped out of the sky and nearly collided with their vehicle. The beast was described as being nearly 10 feet tall with enormous wings and clawed feet. Although the encounter was brief, it frightened the witnesses enough to leave a lasting memory of its appearance. The sighting may have been a precursor to a flap of reports which began three years afterwards farther south, and continue to this day.

Since 2011 a rash of Mothman sightings have occurred in the southern Lake Michigan area and its coastline cities. Reports from Indiana, Illinois, and Wisconsin matching the description of the legendary flying cryptid have become frighteningly common near waterfront settlements, most notably in and around Chicago. A creature closely resembling the Mothman has been spotted throughout the Windy City. From sightings by pedestrians at the crowded downtown riverfront to a spot-on description from a truck driver's encounter near O'Hare International

Airport, reports have continued to roll in over the past decade. In such a large metropolis, several questions emerge regarding the large cryptid beast: where does it nest, is it a solitary creature, and most disturbingly, what does it feed on?

Just over 200 miles southeast of Chicago, on a cold December night in 2018, a farmer and his wife were driving near the Prairie Creek Reservoir on the outskirts of Muncie, Indiana, when out of the corner of his eye the man saw something that made him slam on the brakes. His startled wife peered over the dashboard, attempting to see what had so suddenly spooked her husband. To the side of the road, just above the tree line, she caught sight of a massive humanoid form gliding through the sky.

The farmer, an avid outdoorsman and military veteran, said the creature was unlike anything he'd ever seen. He described it as being roughly 7 feet in length with a bulky, dark-colored body. The bat-like membrane wings did not move as it flew; it seemed to simply glide in a horizontal direction.

In this case, the witness's military background and knowledge of local wildlife made it less likely that his sighting was a simple case of misidentification. He described the creature's movement as "gliding." Most reports of Mothman sightings, from as far back as the original 1960s encounters, state that the cryptid's flight abilities do not rely on the movement of its wings. Almost all witnesses claim to have seen it fly either vertically or horizontally with no perceived motion of the outstretched appendages.

If the presence of Mothman around the Great Lakes isn't enough to make people cast an apprehensive glance skyward, the frightening sightings of a flying creature known as Batsquatch may keep them from venturing out at all. Sighted more often in the Pacific Northwest, and in many cases in regions where Bigfoot encounters are prevalent, this creature made its presence known to the people of La Crosse, Wisconsin, in the autumn of 2006.

That September, two men were driving home at night on a rural stretch of road on the outskirts of La Crosse when they were forced to swerve out of the way of a large airborne beast, which swooped in front of the truck before shooting up into the air, letting out a horrible shriek as it ascended into the night sky. The men described the creature as being man-sized with a dark body, protruding ribcage, and horrifying canine-like face.

They estimated the wingspan to be roughly 12 feet, as they believed it to be larger than the front of the truck.

Sightings continued through the area over the next few weeks, as the creature was spotted on rooftops and in large trees, showing no fear of humans as it terrorized local neighborhoods. A rash of pet disappearances coincided with these Batsquatch encounters. When the weather cooled, the sightings stopped as abruptly as they had begun. Perhaps La Crosse was a stop-off on a migratory pattern for this bizarre flying cryptid as it moved from the rural northern woods to a warmer southern climate.

A creature similar to both Mothman and Batsquatch made its presence known in the summer of 2014 on a rural stretch of highway in Niagara County, New York, near the shore of Lake Ontario. A local man witnessed what he thought was a large eagle swoop in front of his car, blocking out the beams from his headlights as he drove past an old cemetery one night. When the beast landed inside the cemetery gates, he realized it was no bird at all, but something altogether unfamiliar to him.

The driver described the creature as standing between 6 and 7 feet tall with red eyes, short grey fur, and no visible arms. The wings appeared to be membranes, like giant bat wings. This creature was more humanoid in appearance, like Batsquatch, and flapped its wings while flying. Mothman is normally reported to fly without the movement of its wings.

How does one rationalize the sighting of an animal they can positively identify, yet know has been extinct for more than 65 million years? One witness, Jennifer, who lives in Michigan's Lapeer County, has for the past decade sighted what she believes to be a pterosaur, perching in a group of willow trees behind her house.

> "For the past ten years, I've seen what I believed to be a massive bird landing in the far back yard in a group of weeping willows. It was always obscured by the trees, but I couldn't believe how large the wings were," she stated in an interview. "Last year the trees were thinned out and the view became less obstructed. I could see it much more clearly; the wings were brown, no feathers or fur. I saw the back of its head, and I know it sounds insane, but it has the shape of a pterodactyl's head."

Jennifer went on to describe the area as being somewhat wooded with a spring-fed pond behind the neighboring house, backing up to a large cornfield. All of her sightings have been solitary, occurring in the spring, and all during daylight hours. The fact that these annual encounters occur at roughly the same time each year suggests the possibility of a migratory pattern.

Is it possible pterosaurs still exist in limited populations? As strange as Jennifer's encounters may sound, sightings of pterosaurs are still reported across the country and around the world, including recent reports from Texas, Georgia, Washington, and Oregon. It may be just one more of the airborne anomalies that has yet to be identified by science, startling frightened onlookers as they cut through the skies above and became another entry in the realm of anomalies known to the Great Lakes.

Haunted Road Trip

Lakeside Hauntings

THIS BOOK IS A FANTASTIC JOURNEY INTO ALL THINGS WEIRD AND EERIE ABOUT THE GREAT LAKES REGION. We share tales of sea serpents, UFOs, woodland creatures, fairies, gnomes, ghost ships, and more. However, we could NOT do a book without dedicating an entire chapter to haunted locations. After all, it's where we started this crazy journey – from when we were kids running to our local library to read about everything spooky and weird, to the beginning of our adult life and the formation of the Upper Peninsula Paranormal Research Society in 2000. This entire journey is highlighted in our inaugural book, *Yoopernatural Haunts: Upper Peninsula Paranormal Research Society Case Files.*

There truly is nothing better than a good ghost story. As a child, as much as I loved reading about Bigfoot, The Loch Ness Monster, and UFOs, nothing held my attention more than a ghost story. This chapter will cover a few of our favorites. So, pack your bags, fill up the gas tank, and let's hit the road for this ghostly road trip of lakeside hauntings.

Our first story begins on the banks of Lake Michigan in a town known for its shopping, professional sports, food, music, and nightlife. Not just the nightlife of bars and clubs, but also the nightlife that lends itself to an unseen world.

Chicago boasts a population of over 2.7 million and a stable of haunted tales to match. If you want to get the real taste of Chicago hauntings, I suggest books by Ursula Bielski. Her series on haunted Chicago and other topics are enjoyably written and will give you an excellent introduction to Chicago's ghosts. Or, if you are in Chicago and want a front row seat, you can jump onboard Ursula Bielski's Haunted Chicago Bus Tour, "Chicago Ghost Tour."

SS *Eastland*

On the east side of Chicago lies the Chicago River, a waterway leading to Lake Michigan. One of the many bridges spanning the Chicago River is the Clark Street Bridge, the location for the *Eastland* Disaster in 1915. But before we get to that story, let us go back in time a bit farther.

The SS *Eastland*, owned by the Michigan Steamship Company, was officially launched into its life among the Great Lakes on May 6th, 1903, calling Chicago its home. The *Eastland* was a passenger ship used for tours and destinations along the Great Lakes, mainly between Illinois and Michigan. Her skinny, sleek design allowed the *Eastland* to cut through the waters at high speeds, quickly earning the name, "Speed Queen of the Great Lakes."

However, the very design that allowed her to move quickly through the waters would also be her undoing. Very early in the career of the ship, and multiple times throughout her life, the vessel would have issues with listing. It would tilt too far to one side, or the other, with loading and unloading of heavy cargo or a large number of passengers. The ship would again fight this issue on the morning of Saturday, July 25th, 1915, with deadly consequences.

The Western Electric Company was throwing its annual company picnic. It was an event that employees looked forward to all year. It was a special occasion where employees and their families dressed in their best outfits for the day, to be spoiled by the company. This day's destination was Michigan City, Indiana, across Lake Michigan. The Western Electric Company hired five passenger steamships to handle the large crowd. The *Theodore Roosevelt*, the *Petoskey*, the *Racine*, the *Rochester*, and the ill-fated *Eastland* were all docked in the Chicago River, ready for boarding.

As a possible bad omen, it started to rain at 6:30 am, as the passengers began to board the *Eastland*. They quickly ran to one side of the boat to wave to onlookers and friends on the dock. Immediately, the ship began to list. The crew tried to fight the list by allowing water into the ship's ballast tanks. As more and more passengers came on board, the issue continued, and the ship began a slow, methodical pendulum motion. The crew fought this issue for almost an hour until around 7:25 am when the list to port became so bad that passengers, and some crew, began to jump in the water. By 7:30 am, the *Eastland* had made one final jolt to port and rolled entirely on its side in the Chicago River, in 20 feet of water.

At capacity that morning, the *Eastland* had 2,572 passengers on board. By the time the disaster was over, 844 people, including 22 entire families, lost their lives, in 20 feet of water. History records this disaster as the most extensive loss of life in one boat wreck on the Great Lakes. Most who died were already down in the hull of the ship, trying to warm up and dry off from the early morning rain.

The bodies pulled from the ship were hauled en masse to a makeshift morgue at the 2nd Regiment Armory building on nearby Washington Street, where the corpses of victims were assigned numbers and laid out in rows of 85, where they awaited identification by family members and friends. By July 29th, all remains in the armory had been claimed with one exception; a young boy, #396, who the police nicknamed Little Feller, was the last resident of the once full morgue. When his body was moved to a local funeral parlor, a neighborhood child caught a glance of Little Feller and recognized him as his friend, 7-year-old Willie Novotny. When authorities searched for Willie's family, they discovered both parents and his 9 year old sister had also perished in the disaster, one of several entire families to be claimed by the *Eastland* disaster. With the sudden loss of life that day, and the overwhelming energy of sadness and despair, it is no wonder the Second Regiment Armory building was never the same after that fateful weekend.

The Second Regiment Armory

In its history, The Second Regiment Armory would eventually become a very popular building for tourists around the world. It became the home of Harpo Studios, the company owned and operated by Oprah Winfrey, and the location of her popular talk show. Harpo Studios would eventually move to California, but for many years, Oprah, and Harpo Studios, called Chicago home.

Immediately, crewmembers and workers in the building started talking about strange events at the studio. Many of the classic tales of hauntings were reported. Footsteps heard, but no one seen, bone-chilling cold spots, doors opening and closing, and old-time music throughout the building, with no obvious source. Often a woman, or child, was heard crying throughout the building. A little girl was often seen running down the hallway to a vending machine, stopping in front of it, only to disappear.

A former security guard shared his story. Late one evening, his office phone rang. A troubled worker a few floors up, complained about hearing a large gathering of people right outside her door, talking loudly and sounding upset. Thinking some co-workers had returned, she opened the door only to see no one there. Confused, she shut the door and went back to her desk to continue working. Soon, the loud voices began again. The sounds were directly outside her door. She believed she even saw shadows moving across the light showing underneath her door. Something did not feel right, and that's when she called the security guard. She asked the guard to please come up and escort her out of the building. As the security guard made his way up to her office, he carefully checked each floor to make sure no one had come in. He eventually reached the worker's office and explained to her that there was no one on her floor, or on the other stories leading up to her office. She could not get out of the Harpo building fast enough, that evening.

Of all the stories and experiences in the building, the most famous is the "Grey Lady." She is seen as a full-body apparition throughout the entire building, mostly whisking quickly past people in the hallways, or standing solemnly on the balcony of the studio where *Oprah* was filmed. Eyewitnesses report that she wears a long grey dress and a large hat. Many people describe the style of clothing as what would have been worn on the day of the *Eastland* disaster.

Oprah only spoke of the hauntings at Harpo Studios once on her show during a taping in 1996. Although she has stated before that she believes in ghosts, and often had psychic mediums on the show with her, she never liked to talk about what happened within the walls of Harpo Studios.

Once Harpo Studios moved to California, the building was eventually bought by McDonald's to be used as headquarters office space. No reports coming from Happy Meal land, yet, on hauntings.

Site of the *Eastland* Tragedy

The location of the old Second Regiment Building is not the only haunted place connected to the *Eastland*. Take a walk along the Chicago River. The city has done a tremendous job putting in the beautiful Chicago River Walk and installing a memorial to all those who lost their lives that day. As you approach the area between Clark Street Bridge and the LaSalle Bridge, stop and pay your respects. You are standing in the area of the disaster. Many witnesses claim that, late at night, you can still hear the screams.

So, whatever became of the SS *Eastland* after July 25th, 1915? Later that same year, the ship was sold to the United States Navy, where it became a gunner boat, used mostly for training. It was renamed the USS *Wilmette*. It would stay in service with the U.S. Military for quite a while before it was decommissioned on November 28th, 1945. About a year later it was sold for scrap on Hallowe'en 1946. A rather fitting end for this ill-fated ship.

A Connection with the Spiritualist Movement

Our next story takes us from the western shores of Lake Michigan to the easternmost Great Lake. On the belly of Lake Ontario sits the City of Rochester, New York, six hundred and two miles from our first story in Chicago. Rochester can arguably fight for the title of the birth of Spiritualism, duking it out in the ring with Lily Dale, NY, and Hydesville, NY, which no longer exists, but at the time was a part of the township of Arcadia.

Lily Dale can make its claim as it is the location of the Lily Dale Assembly, home for mediumship and spiritual healing. Hydesville is the historical home of the Fox sisters, who were credited with sparking the age of spiritualism. However, many believe the Fox sisters' trip to Rochester, NY, which made them popular, was the actual beginning of Spiritualism.

Corinthian Hall

In 1849, architect Henry Searle constructed what many believe was the jewel of upstate New York, the Corinthian Hall. At the time, the hall was owned and operated by the Rochester Athenaeum and Mechanics Association. It was the premier lecture hall, seating 1,200 people. The Hall also housed an impressive law library, reading rooms, and state-of-the-art office space. It was initially to be named the Athenaeum, after the original 1829 Athenaeum Hall it replaced. On the eve of its christening, the name was changed to Corinthian Hall, inspired by the Corinthian columns on its main stage.

Corinthian Hall soon became the place for social elites to come together for amazing programs and speakers. It hosted activities as diverse as boxing and gymnastic demonstrations, discussions on poetry, and Shakespearean readings. Celebrities and the who's-who of their time spoke to sold-out crowds. Personalities such as operatic star Jenny Lind, suffragette Susan B. Anthony, Charles Dickens, Lincoln Cabinet member William H. Seward, famed showman P.T. Barnum, and abolitionist Frederick Douglas, all lectured or performed at the Hall. Douglas became quite fond of Corinthian Hall, where he spoke many times and where he delivered his famous keynote address, "What to the Slave is the Fourth of July?" on July 5, 1852.

Of all the fantastic speakers and presentations that graced Corinthian's stage, perhaps the strangest happened on the evening of November 14th, 1849, when Catherine (Kate) and Margaretta (Maggie) Fox took their place in Corinthian and Spiritualism history.

****

In 1848 two young sisters in the town of Hydesville, NY, were about to catch the attention of family, then neighbors, then a country, and eventually the world, by claiming to be able to speak with spirits. The family lived in a rumored haunted farmhouse, a historical landmark that still stands today. One night in late March, the family was startled to hear loud knocks coming from within their home, and the sound of furniture moving. Kate Fox, ten, and Maggie Fox, fourteen, tried to communicate with the spirit that the family believed was in their home. A few days later, the Fox sisters created a system to communicate with the entity by having differing numbers of knocks represent "Yes" or "No," and letters of the alphabet. Soon they were having full conversations with the being they were calling "Mr. Splitfoot," another name for The Devil.

Soon, excitement started to grow in the small community, and neighbors traveled to see the young sisters who could talk to the dead. Eventually, the crowds became too much. The parents sent Maggie and Kate to Rochester to live with family. Maggie moved in with their brother David, and Kate with their sister Leah, now married with the last name Underhill. However, instead of receiving peace and quiet, the knocking and communicating followed the two younger sisters to Rochester.

The oldest sister, Leah, saw opportunity and stepped up to be the girls' manager. She introduced them to the world as the amazing Fox Sisters who could communicate with spirits. On the night of November 14th, 1849, the sisters took the stage at Corinthian Hall for the first of three presentations. According to author and medium, Rev. Tim Shaw, in his co-authored book, "*Haunted Rochester: The Supernatural History of the Lower Genesee*," he wrote, "The following announcement was published in the pages of the *Daily Advertiser*. 'Doors open at 7 o'clock. Lecture to commence at 7 ½. Admittance 25 cents; 50 cents will admit a gentleman and two ladies.'" The first demonstration attracted 400 of the city's curious. As was the norm of the era, this form of entertainment also brought along with it many rowdies ready to cause mischief at the first opportunity.

Shaw went on to say, "It must have been quite a presentation. First, Eliab W. Capron presented a lecture embracing the full history of the rise and progress of these strange manifestations. Next, the sisters were paraded out to the enjoyment and catcalls of the audience. In order to accomplish this phenomenon, the girls would sit or stand quietly; sometimes, they were roughly held or bound by selected audience members to prevent trickery. When the spirits were ready to speak, a loud, sometimes metallic, knocking sound would be heard. Some in the audience claimed that they emanated from the walls while others from the ceilings and floors. During the three days of demonstrations, public committees examined the girls for any deception. Nothing was found."

By the end of the third night, the Fox sisters had become a modern-day version of rock stars. Men rushed the stage to get an up-close look, and to see for themselves the sisters who could talk to the dead. Local police were on hand to give the Fox sisters a safe escort out. Newspapers wrote of their abilities, and people came from all over to see them. These three nights at the Corinthian were the first time people paid to see what became the birth of the Spiritualist Movement.

The Fox sisters would make a living of traveling the world, showing their ability. Through this time, many "experts" came forward to examine their work. For every expert who said they were fake, another stated that they found no trickery. For every "friend" that came forward to say they knew all the tricks the girls used, another would come forward and support the sisters' authenticity. It was a never-ending rollercoaster of claims, but through it all, the Fox sisters rode the fame. However, living the rock star life, sadly, Maggie and Kate would become addicted to the drink.

As alcoholism took hold of the two younger sisters, they eventually had an epic falling out with their older sister, Leah, in 1888. In search of money and wanting to get back at their eldest sister as much as possible, Maggie and Kate traveled to New York City, where it was reported they were offered a substantial amount of money to give a written, sworn statement exposing their methods.

Maggie told the story before 2,000 people and rocked the Spiritualism world. Kate was there to support her sister. Part of the account read, "Mrs. Underhill, my eldest sister, took Katie and me to Rochester. There it was that we discovered a new way to make the raps. My sister Katie was the first to observe that by swishing her fingers, she could produce certain noises with her knuckles and joints and that the same effect could be made with the toes. Finding that we could make raps with our feet – first with one foot and then with both – we practiced until we could do this easily when the room was dark. Like most perplexing things when made clear, it is astonishing how easily it is done. The rapping is simply the result of perfect control of the muscles of the leg below the knee, which govern the tendons of the foot and allow the action of the toe and ankle bones that are not commonly known. Such perfect control is only possible when the child is taken at an early age and carefully and continually taught to practice the muscles, which grow stiffer in later years. This, then, is the simple explanation of the whole method of the knocks and raps."

One year later, in November 1899, Maggie would try to rescind her statement in a formal letter.

Those who believe the Fox sisters were a hoax say the confession is all the proof you need. Others, who believe in the ability of the Fox sisters, say Maggie's recantation is sufficient. They believe that it was her alcoholism and need for money that led her to make the false confession in 1889. Either way, Maggie and Kate Fox, directed by their sister, Leah, started a movement that is still thriving today. Leah died one year later, on November 1, 1890, at the age of 77. The youngest, Kate, passed away July 2, 1892, at 55, followed by Maggie, on March 8, 1893, at 59. All three sisters are buried in Brooklyn, NY. Leah's final resting place is located at Green-Wood Cemetery, with the Underhill family. Sadly, Kate and Maggie died with no money to their name, but with the help of friends, they were buried together in Cypress Hill Cemetery.

As for the majestic Corinthian Hall? Once the gathering place for the who's who in New York Society, it would slowly fade into history, much like the Fox sisters. Eventually renamed the Corinthian Academy of Music in 1878, it was destroyed by a fire in 1898. It was rebuilt and opened in 1904 under the name of the Corinthian Theater. The doors would close for good in 1928, with its Law Library moved to the local Rochester Library, and the Corinthian taking its final bow that year as it was torn down.

Where Corinthian Hall once stood is up for much debate, even today. According to the Rev. Tim Shaw, "The 1897 city directory gives the address as Exchange Place, which then ran from 33 Front St. west to 20 State St." With no actual address, but only a location, its exact location has become a topic of contention among local historians. At least three different places are said to be where the building stood. One of the less romantic tales is that a parking garage now covers the ground where the Corinthian once stood. However, one place seems to have some spiritual visitors that could offer a clue as to where the Corinthian once stood.

Holiday Inn – Rochester, NY - Downtown

The Holiday Inn Rochester NY - Downtown is located on State Street. Here it seems that some guests have checked in but have never checked out. Along with the typical haunted occurrences, mysterious footsteps, doors opening and closing on their own, and extreme cold spots, two circumstances stand out and have been witnessed many times. Many workers, especially at night, hear a massive cheering crowd. There is also a resident ghost, described as a stunning woman, walking the hallways, dressed in Victorian style clothing such as the Fox sisters would have worn. Why would a woman in period clothing be seen in a modern hotel? Is it possible that the very women who started a spiritual movement still come back to the place where their lives changed forever?

One group, certainly, believes that the Holiday Inn sits on the birthplace of Spiritualism. Rev. Tim Shaw writes, "In the late 1970s the National Spiritualist Association of Churches held their annual convention in Rochester. During a break, some of these delegates gathered in the lounge of the Holiday Inn and drank a toast to Maggie, Katie, and Leah Fox."

By the way, according to recent reviews, the Holiday Inn Rochester NY - Downtown does score a very favorable 4.2 out of 5 in customer satisfaction. Just in case you wanted to make a visit to see if you run into someone from a different time.

Presque Isle Lighthouses

Leaving Rochester, NY, on Lake Ontario, we now head west to the shores of Lake Huron. Five hundred forty-six miles by auto, if you cut through Canada, or 677 miles if you stay in the States, brings you to a peninsula on the northeastern part of Lower Michigan, called Presque Isle. It is the home of not one, but two of the 149 lighthouses in the State of Michigan. Ironically, they stand within one mile of each other, on a strip of land not much bigger.

The newer of the two lighthouses, the New Presque Isle Lighthouse, was built in 1870, came online in 1871, and is still in service today. However, Old Presque Isle Lighthouse, its older brother located about a mile south, is where our story takes place.

In 1838 Congress gave the green light for a new lighthouse to be built on the southern end of Presque Isle, showing the way along the shores of Lake Huron and safe passage to the harbor at Presque Isle, which was used as a haven in the deadly Great Lakes storms. By 1840 the thirty-foot tower was built and in operation. Today it is one of the oldest lighthouses still standing on the Great Lakes. The light and tower remained operational until 1870 when Congress wanted a newer and taller tower constructed on the northern end of the peninsula. The short career of Old Presque Isle Lighthouse had ended after only thirty years in service.

The old lighthouse would stand empty for quite some time until the turn of the twentieth century when the government sold the property to the Stebbins family. The historic structure would stay in the family for 94 years. James Stebbins, in 1995, sold the lighthouse to the Presque Isle Township, which operates it today as a museum and gift shop.

In the late 1970s, the Stebbins family hired George and Lorraine Parris, a retired couple, to work as caretakers of the property. The couple loved the property and treasured the opportunity to care for the "old lady." For the first couple of years, everything went off without a hitch. Then, one late summer night in 1979, the strangest thing happened. The light that had guided many ships to safety, but had been turned off since 1870, turned on and began to spin again! The Old Presque Isle Lighthouse was once more standing guard over Lake Huron, even though no one told her to.

Getting the light turned off was of immediate importance. Having two lighthouses each showing a beacon within a mile of each other could prove disastrous to ships navigating the lake. According to the Parrises, there was absolutely no rational explanation for this. But to make sure it never happened again, George Parris asked the Coast Guard for assistance in dismantling all the working gears and electrical parts in the old tower, only leaving the lens in place for the museum's sake. Just as in 1870, the light was turned off, and the Old Presque Isle Lighthouse stood on Lake Huron's shores, dark.

For years after that, the time at the lighthouse for the managers, George and Lorraine Parris, was everything they had hoped. George became known for his informative and fun tours of the historic grounds. Lorraine loved getting to know all the tourists and visitors. Tourist season after tourist season, the memories and the laughs continued to grow. Sadly, in early January 1992, George Parris passed away of a heart attack at the lighthouse.

At first, Lorraine was not sure she could go back to managing the property for the upcoming season. She could not imagine running it without her husband, with whom she had built so many memories there. As the season grew closer, and with a little time to heal, Lorraine knew she needed to be back at the Old Presque Isle Lighthouse, doing what she and George loved to do best.

One evening, early that summer, Lorraine was driving home after an evening spent with her daughter when she noticed something that made her stop the car and just stare. As she was approaching the grounds, there it was. The light of Old Presque Isle Lighthouse was on, once again! How? Why?

The light could not possibly be back on! Her husband and members of the Coast Guard had dismantled it back in 1979. Lorraine was not sure what to think, or even who to tell, out of worry that people would think she was crazy. She eventually reached out to her son-in-law, who, after further investigation, assumed it must have been a reflection. However, night after night, the light was on. It was much dimmer than if it was running full blast, but there was light. Soon neighbors noticed it, and eventually, the Coast Guard reached out to Lorraine, to explain that it must be turned off because of the confusion it could cause ships. Lorraine politely agreed and stated she would shut the light off if she could!

The Coast Guard eventually arrived to see if they could find the issue, and even they could not. They concluded that the brightness of the light coming from the tower was not enough to confuse the pilots of ships coming through the area. But just to be sure, they removed the bulb and pointed the lens in a different direction. These actions did not help the situation. Multiple tests were done to see if coverings on the tower would stop the light from shining. People drove to all different points to see if they could still see the light. No matter what they did, the light could always be seen. Who, or what, was allowing the Old Presque Isle Light to shine once again over Lake Huron has never been found.

In interviews about the ghostly light, Lorraine has always said it was very startling and scared her in the beginning. But eventually, she came to believe it was her beloved George, still looking over the place they loved so much. In a dramatic way, he was letting her, and everyone else, know that he was still around. After all, when alive, George loved to put on a big show for the visitors at the lighthouse when he gave his tours, and he was a master electrician.

Since George's passing, other events have occurred at the old lighthouse that cannot be explained. Lorraine was in the lighthouse one evening, catching up on work when a bad storm struck. Concerned, she stopped work to move her car closer to the lighthouse, but the door would not open. She saw through the window that two chairs were propped against the door from the outside, blocking her exit. Feeling that this might be a sign that she should stay inside, Lorraine went back to her desk and resumed her work. Just then, a lightning bolt struck the lighthouse, just where she would have been parking her car, had she been able to get outside! Once again, Lorraine believed that George had been looking out for her.

Still Standing Watch

Visitors will often speak of seeing someone up in the tower, standing by the lens, after the lighthouse is closed for the night. One time, the mysterious figure was described as dancing.

On another occasion, a young girl was with her family visiting the lighthouse, and while the family stayed down in the gift shop, the girl took a trip up the stairs into the light tower. When she came back down, she was excited to share with her family what it was like in the tower, and to talk about the friendly man who was up there telling her stories about the place. Knowing she should have been the only one in the tower, she was asked about the man who was with her. Eventually, she was shown a picture of George Parris, and the girl excitedly exclaimed that was the man she was talking with.

Whether it is the spirit of the old lighthouse itself, or the ghost of its former manager, George Parris, (or, as some have speculated, the last keeper to work the light, Patrick Garrity), the Old Presque Isle Lighthouse continues to shine. Perhaps it was tired of literally living in the shadow of its taller, sleeker, younger and better-looking brother, the New Presque Isle Lighthouse.

As a side note, Lighthouse Keeper Patrick Garrity did not die in the Old Presque Isle Lighthouse. But he does hold the record as the longest working keeper for the old light (1861-1870), and the last. In 1871, he and his family moved a mile up the peninsula to become the first light keepers of the New Presque Isle Lighthouse.

The Ghosts of Reder Road

Our last trip takes us back west to the southern shores of Lake Michigan. A little over nine hours and 572 miles later, we arrive in Gary, Indiana. This timing is based on NO potty breaks and ONLY looking at the roadside oddities as we drive by, mind you.

What would a Ghostly Road trip be without a haunted road, right? Well, the haunted road we seek is not in Gary, but rather, just south of it. But this road is so old, and now covered with trees, that it does not show up on a lot of newer maps. So we use Gary as the location point, and from there, the adventure begins!

Eighteen minutes south of Gary lies the small town of Griffith, Indiana, population about 16,000. Within the town lies a road with a dark past. Follow South Colfax Street and keep your eyes sharp. At some point on the route, an old road known as Reder Street (also spelled Reeder and Redar) will connect to Colfax, but it's hard to find. You see, Reder has been closed to traffic since the 1980s due to all the deaths that occurred on it.

A five-mile stretch of road built around 1910, Reder Road was meant to be a working route between neighboring Merriville and an easy way to move product. During the heyday of the American Mafia (1920s-1930s), Reder Road became a popular place for the Chicago mob to bring their victims, whack them, and bury them in the dense, thick woods that surround the road.

In the fall of 1955, Elizabeth Wilson and her boyfriend drove home from a high school dance on Reder Road. The boyfriend suddenly lost control of the car and rolled it off the side of the road. Elizabeth ended up face down in a swampy area, where she drowned. It is said she is buried in the nearby Ross Cemetery. Since that time, many eyewitnesses on Reder Road shared stories of a woman running frantically from the side of the road, directly in front of their car, and banging on the hood. Once the vehicle stops, and before anything can be said, the frantic woman quickly makes her way to the front passenger seat and asks for a ride home, only to disappear a short while later. One eyewitness described the look in her eyes as "dead." Research has found no historical documents to back up the burial of an Elizabeth Wilson in Ross Cemetery, but what is in a name anyway, for those who have witnessed it?

By the 1970s, the location had become known as a very dangerous road. It became a place of drug use and drug deals, and, many believed, Satanic worship, as animal parts were found on the road. Then, in the 1980s, it took an even darker and more sinister turn, as it became a popular place for people to commit suicide. Eventually, the road was officially closed to traffic use, chained off, and left for the eerie dense woods that stood on each side to slowly swallow it through the years.

These days, the road is nothing more than a walking path filled with a dark past, and, as it seems, ghosts. Locals know exactly where to find Reder Road, but visitors have a hard time locating it due to the surrounding thick woods. Many times, visitors believe they are on Reder Road, only to find out later, that they were not. However, whether local or visitor, many on the old road experience weird things.

Many claim to hear screams of terror coming from the woods, screams that seem close by. Others have reported seeing animal parts strewn across the road, as in the past, leaving some to believe that Satanic worship may still be going on in the woods that surround Reder Road. Many eyewitnesses tell of an old white church off in the distance, reportedly the location of a massacre performed by the minister, on his congregation, using poison in the communion wine. It is said that if you listen closely enough, it's not the winds whistling in the trees you are hearing, but the screams still haunting the woods from that dreadful day.

The Mysterious Figure

The one specter that does not seem to have a historical link to Reder Road, but appears often, is the man in the black clothing. He is spotted on the railroad tracks that run near Reder Road—often walking down the middle, slowly toward the witness, with a flashlight in hand. Most witnesses have run away, not wanting to see who or what it is. But a college student tells of how he was out by Reder Road one night, recording nature sounds for a college class, when he saw a figure coming toward him from the railroad tracks. He watched as the figure, carrying a flashlight, slowly approached. Believing it to be a cop, and not wanting to get in trouble if he was not supposed to be there, he approached the figure to explain what he was doing.

As the student got closer to the figure, the light stopped swinging back and forth, and then just turned off. He was glad to have his own light to see down the tracks. He was frightened that someone had turned off their flashlight and was standing in the dark, watching and waiting. As he looked, the figure just disappeared. The student later said, "I ran down the track, thinking maybe someone had fallen and was hurt, but there was nothing when I got to where the form was." It's a moment he says still gives him bad dreams many years later.

I wonder if they make a road sign that reads, "CAUTION. Road Closed Due To Ghosts." If they do, I think I know a place that could use one!

Do yourself a favor and put on your bucket list a haunted road trip of lakeside hauntings of the Great Lakes. We shared just a few of our favorites. Do your research of many more haunted locations. Make sure they are places the public can still go and see, map it out, and hit the open road. I promise it will be an experience you will NEVER forget.

Ghost Ships

IT WAS A PLEASANT NOVEMBER MORNING IN 1914 WHEN CAPTAIN ROBERT CARLSON, HEAD KEEPER OF THE WHITEFISH POINT LIGHTHOUSE, SET OUT TO SERVICE THE FOG SIGNAL. Accompanied by his granddaughter, the two were enjoying the summer-like weather and were looking forward to the sun lifting the stubborn fog over the lake. As they strolled through the yard, Carlson's granddaughter tugged at his sleeve and directed his attention to the lake.

"Grandpa look!" she exclaimed, pointing to a schooner emerging silently from the fog. Despite the lack of wind, the sails on the ship appeared to billow with movement and a red signal light flashed from her mast. Though solid in appearance, something seemed unnatural about the ship, which was much smaller than the modern freight vessels of Lake Superior. The faint tinkling of bells could be heard as the schooner slid back into a fog bank and disappeared.

The girl, amused at the sight of such a strange vessel, turned her attention to her grandfather, whose complexion had become pale white. The captain crossed himself, muttering under his breath that some poor sailors would soon meet their fate. Two days later, during a gale on Lake Superior, the steamer *C.F. Curtis*, along with the schooners *Selden E. Marvin* and *Annie M. Peterson*, all foundered off Grand Marais, Michigan. All 28 crew members from the three vessels perished. Bloated bodies mixed with flotsam from the wrecks floated onto the shore for several days to follow.

A surfman from the Life Saving Station at Vermillion (eight miles west of Whitefish Point) later reported that he wasn't shocked by the tragic events. He recounted how two days prior, he had witnessed a phantom schooner with full sails coast across the windless horizon just off shore, hearing only the muffled sounds of the ghostly crew members and a tinkling bell as the ship sailed past, an omen of imminent disaster.

The appearance of a ghost ship as a portent of doom is a common superstition throughout the world. The most infamous of these is *The Flying Dutchman*, a ghostly sailing vessel that's been sighted since the 1700s along the coast of southern Africa. The legend of the *Dutchman* has become so widespread that the name itself is synonymous with ghost ships around the globe.

The unpredictable weather of the Great Lakes has sent thousands of ships and sailors to the bottom of these cold, freshwater seas. Although some vessels have been lost by human error or faulty equipment, the rapid change in wind and waves has been the primary culprit for many lost ships. A conservative figure from the Great Lakes Shipwreck Museum places the figure of wrecks in the lakes at around 6,000, with the accompanying loss of life over 30,000, while other estimates claim closer to 25,000 wrecks may be scattered across the lakebeds.

With the loss of ships and sailors, along with the superstitious nature that accompanies the maritime trade, it's no surprise to hear tales of a *Flying Dutchman* of the Great Lakes. It is a title bestowed upon several doomed vessels which sailors spy before a torrential storm hammers down, forcing ships to drop anchor. Those captains foolish enough to ignore such an omen risk becoming the next ghostly vessel, doomed to sail the lakes for eternity.

Le Griffon

The original Great Lakes ghost ship is also the first ship lost on the lakes. Constructed in 1679 by French explorer Rene-Robert Cavalier, Sieur de La Salle, *Le Griffon* was the first schooner to commercially sail the Great Lakes as well as the first ship lost on the lakes.

La Salle had the ship built for two purposes; to transport furs, a lucrative enterprise of the day, from the upper to lower lake regions, and to serve as an exploratory vessel in his search for the mouth of the Mississippi River.

The task of building a ship of the *Griffon's* size, 40 feet long and 18 feet wide, in the middle of what was at the time a remote outpost, was not easy. Along with the lack of supplies, La Salle's men had to be wary of the local Seneca Indians, who feared such an imposing vessel being launched into the lakes. Local tribesmen attempted to sabotage the project throughout construction, making at least one attempt to torch the partially constructed hull. Legend has it that when the ship was finally completed and launched in August of 1679, the native prophet Metiomek warned La Salle that his new vessel was an affront to the Great Spirit, and placed a curse on the ship that it would soon be consumed by the lakes it was built to conquer.

Despite the challenges endured during construction, the *Griffon* was complete and ready for service on schedule. Her first voyage was a commercial run, sailing through lakes Erie and Huron, up to Lake Michigan where the crew would load the ship with furs and return to the Niagara region. La Salle ran up great debts while constructing the vessel and was counting on the first shipment of pelts to pay off his creditors.

Even for a ship of *Le Griffon's* size, the Great Lakes were not easily traversed. On the passage through Lake Huron, the weather turned and the crew of 32 men found themselves being tossed in the waves, at the mercy of gale force winds and punishing rains. Huron might have claimed the ship that day, had it not been for their pilot, Luc the Dane. Said to be nearly seven feet tall and of a bad temperament, Luc was not a pleasant character, but he was an experienced mariner. Luc was no stranger to rough seas, having sailed on other large vessels along the Atlantic coast and the Caribbean Islands. His skill at the helm kept the *Griffon* afloat, but La Salle was not impressed with what he perceived as reckless piloting. When an ensuing squabble between the two turned violent, crew members intervened, cooling the situation before a full-fledged fistfight broke out. Once the storm settled and tempers subsided, the crew pushed on to the French outpost at Mackinac Island, where they stopped to receive a scouting report and allow the men downtime on dry land before completing the final leg of their journey.

The *Griffon* was blessed with smooth seas as it glided across the northern shore of Lake Michigan to the tip of Green Bay, near modern day Escanaba, Michigan. It sat docked while the men loaded the ship with pelts and supplies for the return trip to the Niagara region.

Once filled with the cargo of furs, La Salle split the crew: of the 32 men, only 6, led by Luc the Dane, were to return on the *Griffon*, a bare bones staff, but adequate to get the ship back to home port and unload its bounty. The remaining men ventured on to Illinois with La Salle, where they began construction of another ship and awaited the *Griffon's* return.

The next morning, Luc's crew sailed off for Niagara, never to be seen again. Speculation ran rampant as to the fate of the Great Lake's first schooner. The paranoid La Salle was suspicious of Luc, fearing he was in the employ of his enemies. He worried the ship had been unloaded farther up the lake and intentionally sunk, the crew then making off with the goods to rendezvous with another outfit. This theory may have had some merit, as an Indian translator reported a group of Europeans, one matching the description of Luc, being captured by a tribe at the northern end of the Mississippi. However, no other evidence emerged.

Another tale has the ship seeking shelter in a cove on Lake Michigan, where the men were ambushed and murdered by natives, who then stole the cargo and torched the *Griffon*, leaving no remains to be found. Early voyageurs told this story but offered no evidence to back their claim.

The popular theory is that the ship met its fate at the hands of a wicked storm that sprang up the day after it left port. The heavy load of furs may have taxed the *Griffon* beyond the point it could bear, leaving it helpless against an angry lake.

The loss of ship, crew, and cargo proved an enormous detriment to La Salle. He continued his explorations on behalf of France, sailing down the Mississippi River with his remaining crew, until 1687 when, following heated disputes, his men mutinied, killed him, and put an end to his ill-fated expeditions.

In the late 1800s, Missassagi Strait Lighthouse keeper William Cullis was exploring the western shore of Manitoulin Island, Ontario, when he came across an unexplored cave. Inside were the skeletons of several men along with scattered coins and artifacts believed to be of French origin. One of the skeletons was reportedly that of a very large man, leading to speculation that Cullis had stumbled upon the final resting place of Luc the Dane and the doomed crew of the *Griffon*. More support for this story came from a Canadian attorney named Harry Tucker in 1927. Tucker claimed to have discovered the remains of the *Griffon* in shallow water a mile north of Missassagi Strait. His story garnered a great deal of media attention, with news outlets reporting the mystery of the long-lost *Griffon* had been solved. However, upon analysis of the wreckage in question, it was determined to belong to a much larger vessel. Unfortunately, the skeletons and trinkets found in the cave were removed by locals, many of which were kept as souvenirs or lost over the years and could not be recovered for analysis.

More than 300 years later, the true fate of the *Griffon* remains unknown. Many maritime historians believe she foundered in either Lake Michigan or Huron and lies undiscovered in the depths. Every few years, a shipwreck hunter claims to have solved the mystery, stumbling onto an uncharted wreck they believe to be the *Griffon*, yet invariably these allegations end up disproven.

Claims of discovering La Salle's lost schooner may be outnumbered by sightings of its ghost, still sailing the Great Lakes. The year following the *Griffon*'s disappearance, tribal members and settlers reported the ship drifting past the shore of northern Lake Michigan. It was tough to mistake for another ship, as no other vessel like it was on the lakes at the time. These sightings were often followed by severe weather, detrimental to those travelling the lakes and cementing its reputation as a bad omen.

In 1935, crew members of the lake freighter *Lucille* reported sighting a small schooner matching the description of the *Griffon* passing them on Lake Michigan. They attempted to signal the ship, but to their astonishment, the vessel veered off course and disappeared. Later that evening, the *Lucille* was forced to drop anchor and wait out a torrential storm that covered the lake, producing high winds and deadly waves. Sightings of the doomed ship are still reported on lakes Michigan and Huron.

In any given year, a wreck hunter may claim the discovery of a schooner they are "certain" is the *Griffon*. If someday the remains of the vessel are discovered, will her ghost continue to sail the inland seas, or will the *Griffon* finally receive a respite from her eternal voyage?

Bannockburn

The *Bannockburn* has become the Holy Grail among wreck hunters of Lake Superior. The ship, a 245-foot steel steamer, was constructed in 1893 in Middlesbrough, England, for the Montreal Transportation Company of Quebec. It was considered a state-of-the-art vessel, receiving a rare A1 rating from the prestigious Lloyds of London insurance broker. *Bannockburn* ran cargo across the Great Lakes for nine years under the command of Captain George Wood, until one November day, both ship and crew vanished.

As the 1902 shipping season drew near its end, *Bannockburn,* fully loaded with 85,000 bushels of wheat, set out downbound on November 20th, on a scheduled run from Thunder Bay, Ontario, to Lake Huron's Georgian Bay, a port it would never reach.

The fate of the ship is as mysterious as the sightings of her phantom. The last person to report seeing the steamer was Captain James McNaught of the freight vessel *Algonquin.* On the afternoon of November 21st, the *Algonquin* was traveling south of Lake Superior's Passage Island when McNaught spotted the *Bannockburn* running the opposite route. All appeared normal and the captain resumed his duties. However, at next glance, *Bannockburn* had vanished. A scan of the horizon turned up nothing. Captain McNaught assumed that the tailing steamer had made a sharp change of course, moving out of visual range within the short period since he had spotted it; an unlikely action, which would deliberately set the ship off course.

Later that evening, a blizzard kicked up, turning Superior into a churning obstacle of wind, waves, and snow. Vessels were forced to seek the shelter of the closest bay. When *Bannockburn* was listed as overdue for its scheduled passage through the Soo Locks shipping canal, it was assumed she had been forced to drop anchor at the nearest shoreline. When the weather cleared and the ship still failed to arrive at the Locks, search crews were dispatched and freighters on the lake were warned to be on the lookout for the missing vessel. Fearing Captain Wood may have grounded the *Bannockburn* along Superior's north shore, rescuers concentrated on that lengthy stretch of waterfront.

The crew of the steamer *Huronic* mistakenly reported seeing the vessel grounded off Michipicoten Island, just over 100 miles northwest of Sault Ste. Marie. They believed the pattern of lights they had spotted in the fog matched the *Bannockburn*'s; however, no ship was discovered there. Before a retraction could be issued, word of *Bannockburn*'s reported grounding spread, leading the Underwriters Association in Chicago to issue a statement to the owners in Montreal that the ship had been located in fine condition and all crew members were safely accounted for. This report was forwarded to family members of the crew and regional media outlets, causing great confusion among those still searching for the ship. The steamer *John D. Rockefeller* passed through a debris field near Stannard Rock on November

25th, but after hearing the false report of the *Bannockburn* being found, they had not bothered to report it.

On December 12th, a surfman at the Grand Marais Lifesaving Station recovered a lifejacket bearing the name *Bannockburn* floating near shore. This is the only verified flotsam to be recovered. With no new information, the search for the ship was called off; *Bannockburn* was officially listed as lost with all hands.

One legend that surfaces time and again is that an oar from the ship was found on a remote lake front area of Michigan's coastline. Depending on the version of the tale, it is either wrapped in cloth or snagged in a discarded swatch of fish net, floating in a field of driftwood. When the oar is recovered and unwrapped, it is discovered to have the name *Bannockburn* carved into its handle. The more graphic tellings have the letters filled with dried blood. This story can be found in numerous publications on shipwrecks and ghost ships, but is there any truth to the tale?

In 1909, author James Oliver Curwood, who at the time was the top paid novelist in America, published a work entitled *The Great Lakes*, in which he fictionalized accounts of adventures and disasters that occurred throughout the region's history. In a segment dedicated to the *Bannockburn*, Curwood wrote, "Not a sign of her floated ashore, not one of her crew was found. For eighteen months the ice-cold waters of Lake Superior guarded their secret. Then one day an oar was found in the driftwood at the edges of the Michigan Wilderness. Around the oar was wrapped a piece of tarpaulin, and when this was taken off, a number of rude letters were revealed scraped into the wood—letters which spelled the word B-A-N-N-O-C-K-B-U-R-N. This oar is all that remains to-day to tell the story of the missing freighter." Curwood likely knew of the lifejacket recovered from the wreck and dramatized it into this tale for his adventure novel, which eventually blurred into the legend of the bloody oar.

So, what became of the ill-fated ship? One theory holds that Captain Wood attempted to brave the storm in order to keep to schedule, and foundered somewhere in northern Lake Superior, possibly near Stannard Rock. Another, based on the reports from the *Algonquin* seeing the ship there one minute and gone the next, is that the boiler exploded, taking ship and crew to the bottom in an instant. Although not an uncommon fate for steam vessels of that era, none of the *Algonquin* crew heard an explosion, which would have been loud enough to reach them. Was it possible the boiler had indeed exploded, but prior to the *Algonquin* arriving in the area? When Captain McNaught spotted the *Bannockburn*, was he viewing the steel freighter, or the first appearance of its ghost?

If Captain McNaught was looking upon the specter of *Bannockburn*, he was the first of many to encounter Lake Superior's *Flying Dutchman* in phantom form. The season following its demise, several vessels reported the distinct appearance of the three-masted freighter briefly appearing near Caribou Island. Tales are told of the ship appearing with a startling suddenness, forcing vessels out of the path of an unknown obstruction in the lake, saving ship and crew from certain demise; one ghost ship which seems more guardian angel than bad omen.

Rouse Simmons

Normally a season of celebration, Christmas of 1912 was a time of mourning for the Schuenemann family of Chicago. The family patriarch, Captain Schuenemann, always began his winter leave with his ship docked until spring, when the treacherous ice flows of Lake Michigan melted. But this holiday season, the captain was not present. Instead, his family read newspaper reports of scattered Christmas trees washed up on the Wisconsin shoreline, a macabre reminder of all they had lost.

Herman Schuenemann had moved to Chicago in the early 1890s. The Wisconsin-born son of German immigrants had been saving money while working on Great Lakes shipping vessels and felt there were better investment opportunities in the Windy City. It was also more convenient to raise his family there, as many of his cargo loads were delivered to the rapidly growing metropolis, and his downtime between journeys could be spent in his own home with family, rather than in a waterfront boarding house, many of which were located in undesirable neighborhoods.

Schuenemann was one of the most capable pilots on Lake Michigan, commanding several ships throughout his career, making runs to and from ports in Michigan, Illinois, and Wisconsin. It became his tradition to close out each season by running one last load of festive cargo: Christmas trees.

The captain invested a portion of his annual salary in a load of pine and spruce cut from the wilds of northern Michigan, which he brought to Chicago to be sold from the ship, moored at the Chicago River's Clark Street Dock, along with wreaths and garlands which his wife and three daughters assembled. Herman was a well-liked man with a reputation for generosity, who hired the city's poor to help unload the trees and clean the ship for its winter layup. The local media soon caught on to his charity and the tradition of the annual Schuenemann tree lot and bestowed Herman the title "Captain Santa", master of the Christmas tree ship.

Captain Santa was not the only member of the Schuenemann family to earn a living on the lakes. Herman's oldest brother, August, was also captain of a Lake Michigan schooner, and may have inspired Herman to enter the seasonal tree market, as the elder Schuenemann also ended his shipping seasons with a final cargo of wholesale trees. Tragically, in November of 1898 while captaining the two-masted schooner *S. Thal* on its final run of the year, loaded down with trees, August ran headlong into a storm near Glencoe, Illinois, that claimed the ship and all hands. Deeply saddened, yet undeterred, Herman set out for his final run of the 1898 season, collecting the same cargo that had accompanied his brother to the bottom of the lake.

After decades of sailing in the employ of various shipping companies, Herman was approached with a business proposition: a group of investors was interested in purchasing the *Rouse Simmons*, a 123 foot, three-masted schooner that had transported freight across Lake Michigan since it was launched from the Milwaukee shipyards in 1868. The conglomerate offered to bring Schuenemann into the partnership under the condition he would then lease the *Simmons*, allowing him the freedom to contract his own cargos while assuring the owners would receive a return on their investment, a portion of which would also find its way to the captain's pocket. Hence, in 1910 Captain Schuenemann would, for the first time, be in control of his own shipping operation.

Schuenemann and his crew anxiously anticipated the end of the shipping season, and it was no different in 1912. Being such demanding work, the winter respite was a time when the men enjoyed the fruits of their labor and reconnected with family and friends, with whom they had limited contact during the shipping season. As was tradition, Schuenemann would captain the *Rouse Simmons* on its final run of the season then set up shop with his family to sell his cargo of trees to festive citizens of Chicago.

The last week of November, the *Simmons* pulled out of port from Michigan's Upper Peninsula, loaded down with more than 3,000 trees filling the cargo hold. More trees were strapped to the deck, taxing the aging vessel with its final and heaviest cargo of the season. As the ship headed south into Lake Michigan, conditions were calm and welcoming, and the captain hoped for a quick voyage home to end the season.

November has a reputation of being the most dangerous month on the Great Lakes. The weather is known to change abruptly, and many ships have been thrown from calm seas into hurricane-force winds and high waves in a matter of minutes. Such was the fate of the *Rouse Simmons*. As the ship ventured south, the skies turned an ominous black, then opened up, releasing all the fury of a November gale into the schooner's path. Freezing rain was followed by blizzard conditions, producing waves large enough to wash over the ship's deck.

At 2:50 that afternoon, a surfman at the Kewaunee, Wisconsin Life Saving Station reported spotting the ship with its flags flying at half-mast, a universal maritime distress signal, sailing south into the oncoming storm. Deadly waves and heavy snow prevented the station from dispatching their surf boat in a rescue attempt. The surfman contacted the next outpost down the coast at Two Rivers, which was able to launch a powerboat to search the approximate location the *Simmons* was believed to be. However, the growing darkness and increasing snowfall drastically impaired visibility, and they were forced to return to shore. When the storm subsided, no trace of the *Rouse Simmons* was found.

As the holiday season approached, Christmas trees littered the shoreline of Wisconsin, evergreens which had loosed from their bindings on the deck of the *Rouse Simmons*, the only debris to be discovered in the immediate wake of her loss.

The following summer, a bottle washed ashore near Sheboygan, Wisconsin, containing a rolled-up slip of paper, with a note. The letter described a horrible storm washing two men overboard and a badly leaking hull, threatening to give way at any moment. It was a last communication from a doomed vessel. The hastily written note was signed H. Schuenemann.

Aside from flotsam trees, no debris was recovered for twelve years until fishermen on Lake Michigan discovered a wallet wrapped in waterproof oilskin, which was entangled in their net. On further inspection, it contained papers identifying the owner as Captain Hermann Schuenemann. The wallet was forwarded to Chicago and returned to his family.

Mrs. Schuenemann and the girls continued the tradition of selling wreaths and garlands along the Clark Street docks, keeping the tradition of Captain Santa alive and well until the death of his widow. Barbara passed in 1933 and was buried in Chicago's Acacia Park Cemetery. The grave marker bears the image of a pine tree between her and her husband's names. Visitors to the site claim to catch the scent of evergreens permeating the air near her final resting place.

The location of the ship remained a mystery until 1971, when a dive crew verified a wreck resting in 180 feet of water off Two Rivers Point, Wisconsin, to be the *Rouse Simmons*. When the first diver reached the remains, his dive light malfunctioned, forcing a quick return to the surface. No reason for the equipment failure was discovered, but perhaps the captain and crew weren't quite ready for strangers to intrude on their long-silent resting place.

Although the wreck was previously undiscovered, the soul of the ship was not content to remain peacefully on the lakebed. At the end of the 1917 shipping season, newspapers along the Lake Michigan shore reported the strangest tales: during a November storm, sailors from several vessels claimed to have witnessed a schooner matching the *Simmons'* description, bearing tattered sails and flying its flags at half-mast. When they attempted to contact the distressed ship, it simply faded away.

Encounters such as these have become commonplace along the western Lake Michigan shipping route. Legend holds that when a late season gale is about to set in, the *Rouse Simmons* appears as a warning to mariners, an omen to prevent others from disappearing into the depths of eternity as it did so long ago.

SS Edmund Fitzgerald

Modern technology and manufacturing evolution's comforts and safeties give a feeling of superiority over past constructs and, sometimes, a false sense of invulnerability. When the S.S. *Edmund Fitzgerald* entered the waters of the Great Lakes, it was thought to be almost unsinkable. If a ship as solid and powerful as the mighty *Fitz* would not withstand the worst conditions the lakes could throw at it, what chance would any other vessel have to be truly safe?

The *SS Edmund Fitzgerald* was launched in 1958 as the flagship of the Columbia Transportation Company. The 729-foot, 8,686-ton cargo ship was the largest vessel on the Great Lakes at the time, and a crowd of 15,000 spectators turned out to view her entry to the lakes. Unfortunately, the launch did not go smoothly, and old maritime superstitions of a cursed ship fell upon the *Fitz* from day one. Nautical superstition holds that when a ship is christened, any more than one strike to break the bottle reveals a cursed vessel. For the *Fitz*, it took three. Upon the actual launching, shipyard workers struggled with the keel blocks, and when the ship finally slid into the lake sideways, it crashed into the pier, creating a wave which doused many of the spectators, causing one to suffer a fatal heart attack.

Despite the rough start, the *Fitzgerald* was all the company had hoped for. Six different years it set records for tonnage of freight hauled in a single season. By November of 1975, the *Fitz* had recorded 748 round trip hauls on the Great Lakes, most of which ran from Minnesota's iron range near Duluth to the refineries of Toledo and Detroit, logging in better than a million miles in just 17 years. It was a showpiece where the company entertained VIPs and treated guests to trips across the lakes, right up until the month before its demise.

On November 9th, 1975, the *Edmund Fitzgerald*, under the command of Captain Ernest McSorley, cast off on its final voyage. The *Fitz* started out from Superior, Wisconsin, its cargo hold filled with more than 26,000 tons of iron ore, bound for Detroit. Not far into the journey, McSorley contacted Captain Bernie Cooper of the *Arthur M. Anderson*. The *Anderson* was running 10 to 15 miles behind the *Fitz* on the same course, so the two agreed to maintain radio contact, as both feared a large storm system entering the lakes might deteriorate into a much-dreaded November gale. The captains agreed to move to a northerly course where the hills of the Canadian shoreline could provide protection from the developing storm. Unfortunately, the repositioning wouldn't be enough, as one of the worst gales in recorded history bore down on Superior.

Around 3:30 on the afternoon of November 10th, Captain McSorley radioed the *Anderson* reporting damage and a slight list. McSorley planned to slow the *Fitz* down in order for the *Anderson* to move within visual range, Captain Cooper having agreed to shadow the *Fitz* until they reached the relative safety of Whitefish Bay.

Shortly after 5:00 p.m., the storm had worsened and all ships on the lakes were advised to seek shelter. Winds gusted to 70 knots, while waves rolled as high as 25 feet. Although the *Anderson* continued monitoring the *Fitz*, they kept losing sight of her on their radar due to the enormous waves.

At 7:10 that night, Morgan Clark, first mate on the *Anderson*, radioed the *Fitz* to check their course. At the end of their brief exchange, Clark inquired,

"By the way, *Fitzgerald*, how are you making out with your problems?" Captain McSorley replied, "We are holding our own." These would be the final words transmitted from the *Fitzgerald*.

Five minutes following this exchange, the *Fitz* disappeared from the *Anderson*'s radar for the final time. Clark once again attempted to contact McSorley but was met with radio silence. Just 17 miles from the safety of Whitefish Bay, the *Edmund Fitzgerald* had disappeared. Claimed so abruptly, no distress signal could be sent.

Rescue efforts were quick but fruitless, as both Coast Guard and commercial vessels including the *Anderson* attempted to locate any survivors of the *Fitz*. Only two lifeboats and a field of debris were located, with no sign of the 29 men who manned the ship. It had simply been swallowed up by Lake Superior, another victim of the gales of November.

The following May, in a joint effort between the Coast Guard and the U.S. Navy, the wreck of the *Fitzgerald* was identified. Broken in half, the Mighty Fitz lay in two pieces on the bottom of Lake Superior, below 535 feet of water in a cold, silent resting place.

One of the earliest explorations of the wreck site was performed by the dive crew of legendary nautical explorer Jacques Cousteau in the summer of 1980, under the leadership of Cousteau's son, Jean. Upon reaching the wreckage, expedition members were shaken by what they encountered. Although not in the "official" report, divers claimed that upon rounding the front of the ship, they observed strange lights moving through the pilothouse, the last thing one expects to see in the dark depths of Lake Superior. These highly experienced divers rejected speculation that it was merely a reflection and are rumored to have cut their dive short following another such encounter.

On another exploratory mission to the wreck site in 1989, a Remote Operated Vehicle (ROV) was sent to perform an in-depth search of the vessel. Upon reaching the pilothouse, the ROV suffered a complete loss of power and had to be returned to the surface. Upon inspection, no fault could be found with the system, and the vehicle was relaunched. Once again, as it neared the stern, all systems shut down. The *Fitzgerald*, it seemed, was not ready to give up her secrets.

On a windy July day in the summer of 1995, 20 years after the sinking of the *Fitz*, an expedition set out to recover the ship's bell and replace it with a replica bearing the names of all 29 men lost on the *Fitzgerald,* serving as a permanent grave marker for the sailors whose remains were never recovered. The original bell, along with displays honoring the *Fitzgerald* and many other wrecks of the Great Lakes, is now on display in the Great Lakes Shipwreck Museum at Whitefish Point, Michigan.

Ironically, in November 1883, a Great Lakes schooner named *Edmond Fitzgerald* also met a tragic fate. Stranded in a storm on Lake Erie, the seven-man crew made the decision to abandon the ship. When their lifeboat capsized far from shore, all men aboard were lost in the storm. The ship later broke up in heavy seas, victim of another late season gale.

Though the *Fitz* rests on the bottom of Superior, along with more than 240 other wrecks that have gone down off Whitefish Point, its phantom has been reported by the crews of modern vessels passing the area. Several years back, I received a message from a woman who had experienced a run-in with one of the spirits said to haunt the grounds of Whitefish Point, who also claimed sighting a ghost ship which resembled the *Fitzgerald.* "I was down on the beach in front of the lighthouse," the note read. "It was a foggy morning, but when the fog banks thinned, I saw a freighter which was heading straight for the shore! It had a front cabin, and seemed like any other freight ship, but the funny thing was, it was completely silent." The note continued, "I watched it as long as I could, thinking if it didn't change course, it was going to end up grounded right in front of me! All of the sudden, more fog rolled in, blocking my view. When it cleared again, the ship was gone! It had simply vanished."

In 2013, I was investigating the *SS Valley Camp,* a Great Lakes freighter turned museum, along with my research group, the Upper Peninsula Paranormal Research Society, and friends from Metro Paranormal Investigations of Detroit. The ship rests on the waterfront near the Soo Locks shipping canal in Sault Ste. Marie, Michigan, an area the *Fitzgerald* had passed on every one of its hauls from Superior to the southern lakes. Among the displays in the museum are the two wrecked lifeboats from the *Fitz,* one torn completely apart by that deadly November storm.

The UPPRS team was set up near the *Fitzgerald* display. Attempting to contact any ethereal presence, we played in the background the final transmissions between the *Fitz* and the *Anderson,* which had been downloaded onto a team member's phone.

As the session progressed, a two-way radio crackled to life, interrupting the investigation with a request for all members to come to the top deck post haste. As we rushed up the metal stairway, we encountered the rest of the group gathered at the aft deck, staring at the river in silence. The reason for their excitement became apparent: quietly passing in the river was the *Arthur M. Anderson*, the very ship which followed the *Fitzgerald* through that storm so many years ago. The ship whose recorded conversation with the *Fitz* was playing on a loop below deck at that very moment, slipped by just yards away, raising goosebumps on a warm summer night.

The appearance of the *Anderson* was by no means supernatural, yet the synchronicity of the moment was not lost on any of those present. Much like encountering a ghost ship, the experience was a reminder that the Great Lakes hold truths stranger than any fiction. The thousands of vessels and lives claimed by their cold depths prove both an allure and a warning to those brave enough to venture into their untamed waters.

Miscellaneous Mysteries

MANY MYSTERIOUS PHENOMENA AND BIZARRE BEASTS POPULATE THE GREAT LAKES REGION, some too strange to fit into the previous chapters. Monsters that should only exist in horror films, unexplained phantom lights, and creatures that defy categorization; this chapter contains encounters with the strangest of the region's unknown entities.

The Paulding Lights

The trail off Robbins Pond Road near the town of Paulding in Michigan's Upper Peninsula is haunted. Nearly every night, the phantom light of a railroad brakeman may be seen moving through the clearing where the train once ran, warning of a threat that no longer exists. This railroad employee was killed long ago in that very spot; crushed to death as he attempted to warn an oncoming train of a railroad car stopped on the tracks ahead. Since his unfortunate demise, his spirit has been trapped where he died. He waves his light in a vain attempt to avert others from suffering the same tragic fate.

The above is one legend conveyed to the curious to explain the Paulding Ghost Lights. This phenomenon has been occurring for decades in that rural patch of northern Michigan forest. The U.S. Forestry Service posted a marker at the location to show visitors the best spot to view the lights and relate the account of the phantom brakeman. Beneath the carved letters on this wood sign is a cartoon picture of Casper the Friendly Ghost holding a lantern, a sure sign that the Forestry Service doesn't take this tale too seriously.

A second legend tells of a dogsled-riding mail carrier from the 1800's who was murdered while traversing the path of the lights.

In this story, the postman returns every night, taking the form of these illuminations as he attempts to finish his run, still being pulled along by his phantom dogsled team.

Whatever the lights are, they have been a point of contention between paranormal skeptics and believers for decades. At one point, *Ripley's Believe it or Not* offered a hefty reward to anyone able to solve the mystery. No one ever claimed the prize money.

The most common argument claims the lights, which pulsate and occasionally change between white, green, and red, are nothing more than the headlights from oncoming traffic on a highway some four and a half miles away. This road opened in 1966, at the same time many believe the lights first appeared. Students from a nearby university tested this theory. They claimed to successfully debunk the lights as coming from distant automobiles, findings that were published by media outlets worldwide. Could this decades-old mystery have such a simple explanation?

I was giving a presentation at a library one evening when an older gentleman asked if I was familiar with the Paulding Light phenomena. I confirmed I was and asked his opinion of the university's reported findings.

"Nonsense," he stated. "I grew up in that area. The clearing where the lights are seen used to be a lover's lane back in the late '50s, well before that highway was built." He continued, "We would go park up there at night, and those lights would just appear and float in a circle around the cars. It was a great way to get your girl frightened enough to cuddle into you!" If his claim is accurate, not only were the lights present before the road was built, but they behaved in a manner that no headlight beam could.

Another strange occurrence related to the lights is the failure of automobile electrical systems. Visitors who have parked in the area to view the lights have claimed that their car lights and radios shut down. Some even have reported that their engine stalls, only to return to normal operation when the lights disappeared.

In 2010, the SyFy Channel's paranormal investigative show *Fact or Faked* filmed at the location. They monitored traffic on the distant roadway and sent a small plane to do a flyover to recreate the phenomena. The team found that not only was the plane not the culprit, but the lights appeared in the absence of any traffic on the oncoming highway.

Do these observations disprove the university findings?

Are the lights man-made or some unknown phenomena? Or could they be both; headlights through the clearing on some occasions, varying-colored balls of light from an unknown source on others? Until the mystery can be explained beyond a reasonable doubt, I like to think that maybe the old brakeman is still wandering the trail, amused by the curiosity his old lantern causes the living.

The Newberry Stone

One thing I will never forget about writing this book is how I lived through history in the making during its production. The COVID-19 pandemic changed this world's dynamics and will be written about in history books from this day forward. Being a part of history books only comes with life-changing events. What if you had a chance to rewrite a piece of history, reveal something that would rock academia, and cause books to be rewritten?

Here is the piece of history I am talking about. Is it possible that the ancient Minoans traveled from the island of Crete to find their way to the Great Lakes Region between 3000 BC and 1100 BC, during the Bronze Age?

That idea is an argument that continues today, with most historians abiding by the writings in the history books, disputing this possibility. But some believe this was not only a possibility but did indeed happen. Their argument is solid, and to support it, they point to the copper mines of Lake Superior. The incredible history and connection between ancient Minoans and the copper found in the Great Lakes region is a fascinating read and appears in many great books and papers. I encourage you to research the topic. For the sake of this story, what happened in 1896, not 2000 B.C., holds the importance.

On November 28, 1896, an article written in a local newspaper told of an unbelievable find in the Michigan village of Newberry. The article began, "The discovery made a few days ago near here promises to rank in importance second to nothing yet unearthed related to the prehistoric age in this country. Jacob Brown and George Rove, both residents of Newberry, were looking for deer, and in the course of their hunting, startled a mink which made for a swamp nearby and took refuge in a hollow stump. In digging under one side of the stump to get at the mink, they struck stone, which bore evidence of the handwork of man. Becoming interested, they secured picks and spades and unearthed the stones."

In a much later account from a book published in 1966, the author tells of a farmer named John McGruer, who hired two local men to clear 40 acres of his land. In the process, they found buried historical treasures. Regardless of which version happened, we know this much: the findings eventually became referred to as McGruer's Idols and the Newberry Tablet.

What they found on McGruer's farm were three statues ranging from two feet to around five feet in height. They seemed to represent a father, mother, and child; all buried facing east, a position significant to cultures that believed in the Sun God. Along with the three figures was a 19-inch by 26-inch stone tablet with a total of 140 squares. Within most of those squares were symbols that no one understood.

Eventually, the findings were sent to the University of Michigan and The Smithsonian Institute to find answers. Both institutes at that time said they could not make heads or tails of the writings. The University of Michigan went as far as to call it a hoax, basing their claim on a rash of false historic relics inundating the state in the late 19th and early 20th centuries.

As time passed, the objects sat unprotected at the farm of John McGruer, becoming weather-worn and succumbing to further deterioration from kids playing with them.

Eventually, historians studied more of the Minoan culture. With further research into understanding this ancient civilization, their language and forms of communication began to unfold. That's when the Newberry Tablet once again found its way to the headlines. By now, the only way to read the tablet was from photos possessed by the University of Michigan and the Smithsonian. The original writings on the stone were severely deteriorated. It was then that research attributed a possible language to the tablet that stumped academics for so many years. They believed the symbols to be ancient Minoan.

But how can this be? For the Minoans to have been in the Great Lakes region around 2000 B.C., it would mean they were here long before Columbus' arrival in 1492. Long before Leif Erikson and the Vikings, who are believed to have landed in North America around 1000 AD. This claim could rewrite history books.

Trust me; this is one that can keep you up at night if you let it. The Newberry Stone, or Newberry Tablet as it is also known, now sits on display at Fort du Buade Museum in St. Ignace, Michigan. Historians continue to debate its authenticity; some claiming Farmer McGruer and his friends manufactured these pieces in a bid for fortune and fame. Could a rural farmer and two assistants in 1896 create a historical replica that not even professionals at the University of Michigan or The Smithsonian Institute could decipher at that time? And have it backed by research many years later as resembling the *Linear A* language of the Minoans? Considering how little was known of the Minoan culture or its symbolism at the time, it seems hard to believe.

Mineral Point Vampire

Vampire. The word itself conjures images of pale-faced, fanged creatures who once walked the earth in human form, now reanimated in death to stalk the living for their precious lifeblood. I have investigated Romanian castles once inhabited by the legendary Vlad Tepes, the model for the most famous of all vampires, Bram Stoker's *Dracula*, and discovered no evidence of nosferatu. I have searched London's Highgate Cemetery, home to a rash of sightings beginning in the late 1960s and continuing well into the 1970s; again, no signs of a bloodsucker. I may have had more luck had I searched closer to home, but rural Wisconsin had never entered my mind as a prime local for vampire hunting; as it turns out, it should have.

The old mining town of Mineral Point, Wisconsin, with a population of around 2,500, experienced the first encounter with its hometown vampire in the winter of 1981. Officer John Pepper heard rumors around the town of a dark figure stalking the grounds of Graceland Cemetery, but hadn't paid any credence to the stories. Pepper assumed local youths seeking entertainment had made up the story, which spread through the local gossip hounds, and evolved to the current tale, as so often happens in small communities.

When Officer Pepper received a transmission reporting a dark figure wandering the cemetery, he did not hesitate to respond. It was a typically slow March night and investigating the supposed ghoul sighting provided a welcome break in the monotony.

Pepper was greeted by silence as he entered the dark grounds of the cemetery. The fresh snow crunched under his boots and was the only sound he heard. The beam from his flashlight scanned the tombstones, illuminating what he thought was an empty field when out of the corner of his eye, he saw something moving.

Angling the light between two marble monuments, he was startled to see a black-clad figure staring back at him. In front of Officer Pepper stood a tall, thin man with a deathly white complexion, wearing a dark suit and black cape.

The man immediately rushed away from the officer, who gave chase. Running toward the cemetery fence, Pepper was confident he had the suspect cornered when, without breaking stride, the figure leaped over the 6-foot high barbwire fence and disappeared into the night.

The following morning, after dealing with ribbing from his fellow officers over his "vampire" sighting, Pepper and a few deputies from the department returned to the cemetery for a daylight inspection.

Following footprints through the snow, the deputies verified Pepper's report. They also noted that the suspect's tracks ended inside the barbwire where he reportedly jumped the barrier. On the other side of the fence, the snow was undisturbed. The caped man had never landed.

There were no more reported sightings of the Mineral Point vampire for another 23 years, until March of 2004 when authorities received a strange call.

A man wearing a cape sat in a tree near an apartment complex. He also was tall and chalky-complexioned. He would jump down towards people who exited the building. When officers arrived, they witnessed the figure jump from the tree and flee. The officers followed and thought they had the suspect cornered when, once again, without breaking stride, the figure leaped over a 10-foot concrete wall and disappeared.

Four years later, authorities were summoned to deal with the vampire for a third time, when a young couple was attacked while on a fishing date. On July 11, 2008, Brandon Heinz and his girlfriend, Jamie Marker, were fishing at Ludden Lake, a local bass fishing hotspot in Wisconsin's Iowa County, when they came face to face with the ghoul. They reported to police that the man came out from under a dock and began to advance upon the couple. Frightened by his strange appearance and demeanor, the two made a run for the car as the caped figure began to chase them. As the man gained on Brandon, he turned and flung his flashlight, striking the pursuer and buying enough time to reach the car and make a quick escape.

Brandon drove directly to the police station, where the chief dispatched officers to search the lake area for any trace of the man, once again described as tall and pale-skinned, attired in suit and cape.

Officers found no trace of the vampire. The couple's fishing gear was in the spot they'd left it, undisturbed. The flashlight Heinz had hurled at his attacker, however, was never located.

Did a vampire terrorize the town of Mineral Point? The consistency of witness descriptions and multiple police reports suggest that some person or being was stalking the area for almost 30 years. Perhaps the more intriguing question is when he will appear next.

What's in the Skies of Erie, PA?

Erie, Pennsylvania, a town of just over 96,000, sits on the Great Lake bank that bears the same name, midway between Cleveland, Ohio, and Buffalo, New York. The name of the town and lake screams that weirdness should be happening there, and it is!

There are plenty of ghost stories of ships and sailors lost at sea. Lake Erie is the shallowest of the Great Lakes, averaging just 62 feet in depth as compared to the largest, Lake Superior, which averages 483 feet. Science says that it's the shallow makeup of Erie that makes it extremely susceptible to rogue waves that can tower over fifteen feet tall, occurring just moments after the lake was a perfect calm. These waves give credence to the legend of the Sea Hag of Lake Erie and may hide her various sea monsters. It's not just the waters that surround Erie, PA that make it, well an eerie place to be – it's what's happening in the skies above that have a lot of people looking up.

September 24, 1950 was a very dark day for Erie, but it started as a perfect fall morning. The oranges, reds, browns, and yellows of the leaves were everywhere for residents and tourists alike to enjoy. The sky was blue, with just a hint of clouds, and the crisp fall breeze pushed the smells of autumn down every street.

Around noon, the sky suddenly started to turn a weird yellow. People were stopping in their tracks and pulling cars over to watch.

Some reported afterward they thought a storm was rolling in off the lake. One bystander told the press he felt it was an eclipse that he had missed media reports about. By early afternoon, the sky had turned from the hazy yellow to pitch black. Erie, PA, had turned to midnight at 1:30 in the afternoon.

Whatever this was, it was also affecting parts of Ohio, New York, and Canada. Shortly after 2:00 pm, streetlamps were turning on, and the local newspaper had already fielded over two-hundred phone calls. All afternoon sporting events were canceled, and local authorities were trying to calm citizens while seeking answers themselves.

With no reason given by local or state authorities, parents were starting to panic and keep their kids locked inside, worried about them breathing the air. Some residents later reported they thought it was nuclear fallout, and the end of the world was happening.

Then, just as fast as it came, the darkness started to fade. Slowly residents began to see the late fall sun trying to break through, and layer by layer, the night went away.

Eventually, the story that authorities told residents of Erie was that it was caused by a forest fire coming out of Canada. There wasn't a single person who believed that. Report upon report came out of people saying there was never a smell of smoke during any of that strange event. Others said they could see stars in the sky as though it was a clear fall night. But the biggest zinger is that Canada never reported a forest fire of any kind on that date.

So, what happened that day above Erie, PA? One theory is that somehow a specific part of the Great Lakes witnessed a type of timeslip. For those few hours, people observed a different time or space than others – a moment when day shifted to night and then back to today.

If you think this was the only strange sky-event above Erie, you are wrong. Let us talk about UFO's and little green men, or in this case, tall scary men.

In 1952 the United States Government created a program to study Unidentified Flying Objects. The program became known as Project Blue Book. It was the height of UFO paranoia and cold war suspicion. Both the military and Hollywood had Americans looking to the sky in fear.

For twenty years, the U.S. Military continued with Project Blue Book, finally closing this chapter in 1972, claiming that most of the cases investigated had natural causes and rational answers, yet, a handful of those cases remained unsolved in the files.

Case number 10798 was one of those, and its location was Erie, PA.

A group of friends drove over from neighboring New York to spend a day on the beach in Erie. After a day of fun, the sun began to set, and it was time for the group to head back. As they began to leave, their compact car became stuck in the sand at the edge of the parking area. After many attempts at the old-fashioned way of getting a vehicle unstuck, pressing the gas pedal as hard as you can, the group quickly realized they had buried the tire deeper than they realized.

The sun had gone down, and they were assessing their situation when they noticed a strange light in the sky. The object appeared mushroom-shaped with a narrow base and hovered above the group for a moment before landing near a tree line, not far away.

By then, the friends were terrified and were working like crazy to push the car out. That's when they saw a hulking black creature, standing over six feet tall and covered in fur, approaching the car. It was too dark to get a clear look at the being approaching them. The boys who were outside the vehicle quickly jumped in. As the creature approached, it began to scratch and bang on the car, causing the occupants to scream, flash the headlights and honk the horn. With this, the creature slowly retreated toward the tree line, and the craft soon took off.

Shortly after, the police arrived to investigate the commotion. After receiving the full story from the group of friends, they helped free the car and sent them on their way. The cops must have believed their story because the next day, a special team, including members of the U.S. Air Force, assembled to assess the situation. They found strange tracks and indentations in the sand that led directly to the vehicle, strides too long to be made by humans. And there, in a tree branch that would have been above the car, they found hair samples over six feet up. A military lab tested the hair samples—the official diagnosis – unknown species.

So if you find yourself on vacation in Erie, PA, a beautiful place filled with wonderful people, shops, restaurants and beaches, make sure to keep one eye on the water, and the other watching the skies, because in Erie you never know what you may see.

The Superior Healing Vortex

Michigan's Keweenaw Peninsula, which juts out into Lake Superior, comprises the northernmost part of the state. It is a land of deep forests, abandoned mines, and dilapidated remains of company towns. It is also home to a sacred healing vortex that draws thousands of visitors a year, hoping to embrace the natural energies and restorative powers the place is believed to exude.

Allouez Township, population 1,500, lies on the northwest tip of the Keweenaw, on the shore of Lake Superior. It is a land of bitterly cold winters where residents measure the snow in feet rather than inches. Thousands of tourists from all parts of the world visit the township from spring through autumn to enjoy what this outdoorsman's paradise offers.

When searching for recommendations on the Trip Advisor website, one may be surprised to find the top-rated attraction in Allouez to be Prospector's Paradise, a rock and mineral shop located in the remains of an old sawmill just off U.S. 41. It also happens to be the only attraction in Allouez listed on Trip Advisor. The shop itself is only part of the draw; directly behind the building is a plot of land which is said to be home to an old Indian burial ground, and the location of an underground river.

The combination of these natural and spiritual energies is believed to have embedded the area with special powers – a vortex where people from far and wide have traveled to soak in the energies and heal any ailments they may be experiencing.

At the center of the vortex, a place where trees grow in twisted formations, is reputed to be the merging place of two subterranean rivers. Pagans have gathered at this site during the summer months, believing the spirits of the dead can make use of the natural energies from these underground waters to hold open an interdimensional doorway, allowing the healing energies to flow through.

Many consider the existence of such a vortex nothing more than local folklore. However, some believe they have benefited from the healing effects and vouch for its authenticity. Some claim merely spending time at the vortex recharges their energy, both physical and spiritual.

Be it a miraculous cure-all or a page out of local lore, the unspoiled natural beauty of this far north territory makes it worth investigating. Other Keweenaw Peninsula mysteries worth exploring include the beachfront area where an Indian maiden from the distant past calls out to her long-lost husband through the singing sands at BeteGrise and a famously haunted auditorium that once served as a makeshift morgue, The Calumet Theatre. Tie in the numerous sightings of Bigfoot on the Peninsula, and you have a destination ripe for any legend hunter.

The Hodag

Some creatures are so bizarre it's hard to believe they could be native to this planet. The Hodag, for example, measures 7 to 9 feet in length and stands more than 3 feet high. It has razor-sharp teeth, formidable tusks that protrude from the lower jaw, and a bite that can crush human bones. The Hodag had citizens of Rhinelander, Wisconsin looking over their shoulders in the mid-1890s.

Descriptions of the beast, said to inhabit the woods outside of Rhinelander, were first reported in a local newspaper in 1893.

Determined to put an end to the threat, local land surveyor Eugene Shepard gathered a posse of local men to hunt down the creature. At day's end, the men returned with the charred remains of what they claimed to be a hodag. Shepard reported to the local paper that the beast was so mean and nasty that sticks of dynamite were needed to bring it down, hence the burnt carcass.

Eugene once again found the spotlight in 1896, this time for capturing a live hodag. Shepard claimed he'd tracked one to a cave in the woods and hired a group of bear wrestlers who used a hefty dose of chloroform to overcome the critter.

Thousands of people would be able to witness a live hodag, displayed at the county fair with Shepard close at hand to tell the tales of his encounters with the vicious creatures. As word spread, the story of the Hodag was reported statewide, then in national newspapers. This new cryptid was so intriguing; the Smithsonian Institute announced it would send a team of scientists to examine the creature. Hence came the end to the tale of the Hodag.

Upon receiving word of the Smithsonian's impending visit, Eugene Shepard was forced to admit the entire saga had been a hoax.

A known jokester, Shepard had invented the hodag story for the paper, then coaxed friends to play along with the ruse by joining his hunting expedition. Reaction to the story of the dead Hodag had been so fantastic that three years later, Shepard revived the creature with his "live" captured specimen.

His fabricated creature included intricate wires, which enabled him to make the beast move on command, making it appear animated.

Rather than bury this elaborate hoax, the citizens of Rhinelander have embraced their homespun cryptid. The city website boasts Rhinelander as "Home of the Hodag," which is hard to dispute when viewing the giant hodag statue in front of their chamber of commerce. The creature is the mascot for the local high school sports team. Every summer the city hosts the Hodag Country Festival, which brings some of the biggest names in country music to Rhinelander to twang their guitars in honor of one of the most beloved monsters of the Midwest.

Black-Eyed Kids

Black-Eyed Kids, Black-Eyed Children, or BEKS.; no matter the name you call them by, they all have one thing in common, a nightmarish outcome!

In most reports, they appear as children between the ages of six and sixteen. They wear outdated or baggy clothes, often hooded sweatshirts that are too big, pulled up around the head, making it hard to see their faces.

Encounters with the BEKS almost always follow five progressions. First, people notice that the clothes just don't seem right. Next, when they speak, the tone of their voice seems wrong. It is monotonous and emotionless. The third anomaly is their skin; they are pale, almost white. By now, the witness is uneasy and on guard. Fourth, if the person refuses to allow them into their house or vehicle, the BEKS will tell them more aggressively that they must be invited before they can enter. It's the fifth and final stage that sears the encounter into the minds of those unlucky enough to meet Black-Eyed Kids – the moment they see their eyes. Pure black! No white of the pupil, no color of any kind, only absolute darkness.

This is the moment that those who encounter BEKS tell you they felt a fear unlike any they have ever known. They are shocked and paralyzed. They want to run or scream but can't. At some point, their primal "fight or flight" instinct kicks in, breaks the paralysis, and allows them to flee or slam the door.

Many of the reported encounters with Black Eyed Kids happen at the front door of someone's home, or beside their automobile. Meeting a BEK in these unguarded situations further heightens the person's dread and terror.

Who are these BEKS, where do they come from, and what do they want? There are no answers to those questions yet. They almost always travel in groups of two or three and seem to prefer the late-night knock at the front door approach, although some stories tell of them approaching a parked vehicle.

It's still not clear when stories of these children first appeared. Some accounts say as early as the 1960s, others say the 1980s, but most agree that the first publicized account comes from Brian Bethel, a journalist from Abilene, Texas, in 1996. In his statement, Bethel explained how he had pulled over one night in front of their local movie theater. He needed to use the illumination from the theater marquis to write a check. Bethel was so focused on what he was doing that he did not notice the two young boys until one of them knocked on his window. He says the fear that came over him was almost immediate, and he had no idea why.

One of the boys stated that he and his brother wanted to go to the movies but forgot their money. They asked if Bethel could give them a ride home to get their money and that the trip wouldn't take long at all. Bethel remembered them assuring him that they were good kids, and they didn't have a gun. The boy's voice was monotone, which Bethel had picked up on right away, and also wondered why a young boy would volunteer up front that they didn't have a gun. Bethel checked the time, realized that the last show at the movie theater had already begun, and with that, he began to tell the boy's he couldn't give them a ride.

Then they made eye contact. Bethel said he felt like he was going to black out when he looked into the stone-cold black eyes. Gripped with fear, he continued to tell the boys he couldn't drive them. Then the BEK started to become more forceful, stating they couldn't get in the car unless Bethel invited them in. Finally, something told him he had to break his stare, and he did. At that moment, he threw the car in drive and tore out of there, never to see the kids again. Brian Bethel stands behind his story to this day.

The Great Lakes region is not without BEK encounters. One comes out of Minnesota, where an older couple was spending their Saturday night as they always did, the husband watching television and the wife doing her crossword puzzles. Around 10:00 PM they heard a knock at the front door. Both husband and wife quickly looked at each other. An uninvited guest at that hour was something that didn't happen in their nightly routine. The husband put down the television remote and went to the door, turned on the front porch light, and looked out the window. There he saw three kids standing on their front porch.

He yelled back to his wife that it was three kids, nothing to worry about, he would take care of it. He opened the door, and there on the porch stood one girl and two boys. The girl seemed to be the oldest and was the one standing closest to him. All three were wearing hooded sweatshirts and had the hoods up around their heads. It was a chilly night, so he didn't find that to be too odd. But what he first noticed was none of the three were looking at him, rather they were either staring slightly down or to the side.

He asked how he could help them, and the female was the only one to answer. She asked, in a monotone voice, if they could come in and use the phone; they needed to call their mother to pick them up. The man was immediately uneasy with her tone and with how none of them were looking at him. He then noticed their clothes, how old and baggy they looked. He started to ask more questions. Where do you live? Does your mother know where you are? Are you in trouble? Are you hurt? With every question, only the girl would answer, and it was always the same, stating they needed to use the phone, it wouldn't take long, and would he please invite them in.

The longer this went on, the more the fear was rising in him, yet he could not get them off his porch. That's when his wife yelled from her chair, asking if everything was alright. The husband turned to answer his wife, stating he was still talking to the kids, and when he turned back to the children, that's when all three were looking right at him, and he froze. Three sets of jet-black eyes were staring directly at him. He couldn't move or say a word. At that moment, he heard his wife in the other room invite the kids in saying, "it must be freezing out there."

That was the invitation the BEKS needed. The husband, still in shock and fear, stood there as he watched the three walk by him and into the house. The moment his wife screamed, he was able to snap out of his paralyzed state. He ran into the living room, fearing what he was going to see. To his surprise, all he saw was his wife looking at him with a terrified expression on her face. She explained that three things went by her and walked right upstairs. On the way by, one looked at her. She told her husband that she had never seen or felt anything like she did at that moment.

The husband reached for the phone to call the police. As he spoke with the police, they heard footsteps coming down the stairs. The couple could only stand and watch as the trio slowly walked toward them. As they crossed through the living room, the girl told the couple that they had done what they came to do, and they left through the front door. The accounts of the night are from the police report.

****

Another BEK story from the Great Lakes Region comes from a small town in Wisconsin, near the western shores of Lake Superior. For the safety and privacy of the family, names and locations have been changed.

What began as a typical summer day in 2001 for Sally and her son, Steven would end in complete horror. The late July afternoon in small-town Wisconsin near Lake Superior's Western shores was an oppressive one, and Sally had taken her eight-year-old son to the lake for some swimming to cool down. Sally and Steven would enjoy the calm lake while Dylan, Sally's Husband, and Steven's Father would be back home taking care of the "Honey-Do" list.

As the afternoon wore on, Sally retired to the beach to read while Steven stayed in the water. It was then that she noticed three young children about thirty yards away. Even though the temperature was pushing into the high 80's that day, these three were standing near the shoreline wearing hooded sweatshirts! "I thought I imagined it at first," Sally told me. "I was sweating just sitting there in my bathing suit, and here are three young kids just standing there with hooded sweatshirts on with long pants and shoes. They couldn't have looked more out of place if they tried." When mom and son had first arrived at the beach, it was full of other families enjoying the beautiful Lake Superior Waters. Now, as Sally looked around, she noticed almost all the other families had left, other than a group that was currently packing up their gear to head out.

"I looked down at my watch, and it was getting late enough in the afternoon, and with us being the last ones to be there, other than those three kids just standing there, I was getting creeped out and ready to go." Sally quickly called Steven to get out of the water, and it was time to go home. After about five minutes of fighting with an eight-year-old who was not ready to call it a day, Sally finally won the argument—the entire time keeping an eye on the three children in the hooded sweatshirts still standing the same distance away. One of them had turned and was looking in their direction, while the other two continued to stare out into the lake.

In record time, Sally had their belongings packed, and they were heading to the path that would take them from the beach to the roadside park where the safety of their SUV awaited them. Before she took her last step off the beach and on to the path, Sally looked back. "I remember vividly looking back one more time toward the three kids, and all three were still standing in the same place, but this time all three were looking our way. I never pulled Steven down a path as fast as I did that day!"

The path was about a quarter mile through the forest, lined with picnic tables for families to stop and enjoy a meal. It was the only path to get to the beach from the roadside park, and Sally had passed no one on the way there, and no one had passed them. "The sun was still shining, and I could see my vehicle through the trees. I couldn't get to it fast enough."

As Sally and Steven emerged from the tree line and headed for their vehicle on the other side of the parking lot, Sally quickly realized they were now the last to leave. She then promptly noticed movement coming their way. Sally turned to her right, where the three kids from the beach were now standing five feet from her. "I froze! I was stunned. There is only one path to get from the parking area down to the beach. I know we left the beach before them, and NO ONE passed us on the way up. Yet, there they were, staring at my son and me!"

It felt like an eternity before Sally could get anything to come out of her mouth, and the kids just stood there, looking at the ground. Steven too, just stood there, saying nothing. Finally, Sally muttered the words, "Can I help you?" One of the boys finally spoke. "We lost our phone, and we can't call for a ride. Can you give us a ride to the gas station so we can call home?"

"NOTHING!" Sally said in our interview. "There was NOTHING in his voice. It was as boring and monotone as anything I have heard!"

Sally was frozen. Fear grabbed her and controlled her. She knew something was wrong, but she couldn't move. Until she heard, "Mommy, what's wrong."

"It was that moment that I snapped out of it. Hearing my child's voice made me realize that the fear I was feeling, I had to protect my son from whatever was making me feel that way. Nothing else mattered at that moment."

Realizing she was cut off from her vehicle's passenger side, she grabbed her son by the arm, quickly moved him to the driver's side, opened the back seat, and shoved him in. "As I was getting into the driver's seat, I heard another voice ask if they could have a ride. I screamed NO, slammed the door, and took off as fast as I could. I almost hit them as I backed out, and I watched all three standing there in my rearview mirror. At that moment, I first saw all of their eyes, as they were staring straight at me. Pitch Black! All three of them had PITCH BLACK EYES! I tore out of there as fast as I could!"

"I must have been shaking, and I might have even been crying because Steven quickly asked me again what was wrong and who the boys were. I came up with a story about how they were older boys just trying to scare us and that I was a little shook up, but we were now OK. He asked me again if I was OK, and I assured him again. This time it must have worked because I remember hearing him humming to himself, and I knew then the ordeal was out of his mind, and that allowed me to relax a little and try to figure out what just happened."

As Sally continued to drive and figure out the ordeal they just went through, she realized she was still shaking and feeling a little lightheaded. She decided to stop at a nearby restaurant where she and Steven could grab a bite to eat, giving herself more time to relax and put things more into perspective. It would also give her a chance to call home and explain to her husband, Dylan, what just happened.

After a phone call home to Dylan, Sally sat there, watching her son polish off a plate of chicken fingers and fries. Usually Dylan had a way to make bad situations seem better. But this time he didn't quite seem to grasp what she was saying. Even so, Sally felt much calmer about everything and felt ready to get home.

As they were pulling out of the restaurant's parking lot, Sally looked to her left to make sure traffic was clear. But what she saw made her blood run cold! "Standing off to the side of the parking lot were two of the three kids I saw at the beach. I sat there and just stared as the two stared back at me." The feeling of dread came washing back over Sally, and the fight or flight kicked in as she floored her SUV much harder than a family vehicle is meant to go.

Immediately Steven was asking what was happening, and this time the situation brought him to tears. Sally was driving as fast as she could. All she wanted to do was to be with Dylan, in the safety of their home. She was so frightened and confused, all while trying to keep her son calm, Sally did not notice how low her vehicle was on fuel. She still had a twenty-minute drive home, and by the time she saw the gas gauge, there was no way they were making it home without stopping to put some gas in the tank.

Sally soon came to a gas station and quickly pulled in. "Stay in this car, DO NOT GET OUT FOR ANY REASON," she told her son. She ran to the other side of the vehicle to begin pumping when she saw the sign that read, "Pre-Pay only. Please see attendant inside."

"You have to be kidding me!" Sally screamed, before she noticed the gentlemen staring at her at the next pump. She quickly ran into the store, paid for ten bucks in gas, knowing it would be quick to get that into the tank, and prayed it would be enough to get them home. She ran out the door to the car and put in ten dollars' worth of gas, and ran to the driver's side to get in. As Sally put the key in the ignition, she looked in the rearview mirror to see how Steven was doing, except it wasn't Steven she saw in the mirror.

There, staring back at her, was one of the kids she had seen at the beach, then at the restaurant parking lot!

"My stomach crawled right up into my throat. I wanted to puke, seeing those stone-cold black eyes just staring at me. I screamed and whipped my head around to make sure my son was OK."

As Sally quickly scanned the back, there was Steven, who had slid over behind her seat, and next to him, the Black-Eyed Child. "Steven.... are you OK? What's going on? Who is this?" Steven answered, "He's lost, Mom. He came to the window when you went inside and wanted to know if we could give him a ride. I said we would help him. What's wrong, Mom? Why do you have that look on your face?"

Sally threw open her door without hesitation, jumped out, yanked open Steven's door, and pulled him out with equal force. "MOM! What is going on? You are hurting me," yelled Steven. Sally pulled her son into the gas station and called her husband. Her husband answered, "Hello?" "Dylan," whispered Sally. "Dylan, I need your help!" "What," responded Dylan. "I can barely hear you. Are you OK?" "No... NO, I am not," answered Sally. "Please, Dylan, don't ask any questions right now and get in your truck and haul ass to pick Steven and me up at the gas station on the corner of 5th and Robertson... NOW!"

From the tone of her voice, Dylan knew something was wrong and without hesitating, jumped in his truck and hitting the road. Fifteen minutes later, he picked up his wife and son. Sally's car sat empty at the gas pump by now yet Sally never saw the Black-Eyed Kid get out or leave. After explaining to her husband that she did not want to drive home, Sally got the OK from the gas station attendants to pull her car to the side of the building and leave it overnight, and they would pick it up the next day. Dylan, Sally, and Steven were now all in the truck heading home, and Sally now had the daunting task of explaining to her husband what just happened that afternoon.

By the time they got home, and Steven fell fast asleep on the couch from exhaustion, Dylan and Sally were arguing. The ordeal of the afternoon was not computing with a husband who considered himself to be levelheaded and certainly DID NOT believe in the boogeyman or ghosts!

"Dylan never believed me," said Sally. "He didn't believe me that day, and he would never lend an ear when I needed to talk about it in the following days, months, and years. As time went on and that nightmare would never leave my memory, I started to resent him for it.

"Steven seemed to have formed some amnesia about the entire event. My doctor said that it is normal for young children to block out an incident that could be traumatizing. He says he doesn't remember a thing from that day, other than some brief moments of remembering being in the water and swimming.

"I never did see those children again, but their faces, their clothing, their eyes are as fresh in my memory today as they were that day. I close my eyes, and they are there. Even though I haven't seen them since that summer day, I wait to see them at any moment. Our lives have never been the same since that day. Shortly after, we lost two beautiful golden retrievers to a rare cancer form that dogs hardly get. Within a month of that, our cat went missing and never came home. A month later, Steven started showing signs of aggression and depression, and we had to have him start seeing a doctor. He is still dealing with the same issues today, as an adult, and still remembers nothing from that day. The distance between Dylan and I continued to grow, and six years after the incident, we divorced.

"I live alone now, with only memories of the perfect life we had before that day and how it all fell apart after seeing the Black-Eyed Kids. I have since done as much research on them as I can find, and all I can conclude is the moment it all changed for us was the moment my son let it into the car."

To this day, Sally and her son still have a relationship, albeit strained, and Dylan is entirely out of the picture. Sally has shared her story a few times, hoping she can help just one person, but she often does not talk about it.

Black Eyed Kids. Who, or what, are they? Are they from another dimension, or another planet, or even from one of the levels of Hell? All three are theories, but the truth is, we don't know. Their origin is as shrouded in mystery as is their plan and what they want. But this much we know – if you hear the late-night knock on the door, or the startling tap on your car window, don't answer the knock or look out the window. It's the best advice we can give, for now.

Tales From the Creaking Door

"WELCOME INSIDE CREAKING DOOR PARANORMAL RADIO," words heard on every podcast created by the authors of this book since it debuted on December 23, 2014. Tim Ellis and Brad Blair wanted to take their love of everything strange to the masses and creating the Creaking Door podcast gave them that opportunity.

Launching a podcast was something the two aspiring authors had wanted to do for quite some time, but the time or the place never felt right. Then, in 2013, a podcast producer from the Detroit area approached them at the annual Michigan Paranormal Convention. The producer asked the two if they had ever thought of doing a show based on the paranormal and the weird. He said it would be the perfect fit for his group of podcasts already on their platform. Of all the shows they hosted, none covered the topics Tim and Brad loved. They knew this was finally the right time and place and jumped at the opportunity. Now, six years later, Creaking Door Paranormal Radio can be heard around the world on iTunes, Google Play, Spotify, and Stitcher.

The show consists of interviews with the biggest names in paranormal television, authors, and speakers covering topics from ghosts, UFOs, cryptids, serial killers, and everything in between. The show also features paranormal news segments and the ever-popular mailbag. This last segment allows the listeners to be a part of the show by submitting their true stories of the strange and macabre. Some of the stories make the show, some don't, but all hold a special place with the two hosts. What follows in this chapter are a few of their favorite stories submitted from the Great Lakes region; stories that sent a shiver down their spines.

We now present to you, "Tales from the Creaking Door."

The Radio Remembers

Hi, Guys, I found your show last month when you had John Zaffis on as a guest and loved it! I've been listening to your past episodes since then and look forward to new ones. I want to share something I went through back in the 80s and get your thoughts on it.

I grew up outside of Cleveland, Ohio, and the summer after I graduated high school, my parents retired from jobs they held at a local factory. They both looked forward to getting out of the city, and just before retirement had purchased a small party store near a resort on Lake Huron. There was a small two-bedroom apartment above the store, which was to be their home during the summer months.

The storefront had been closed down since the previous owner, whose family had founded the business in the 1940s, left the area two years prior. My parents loved the idea of owning their own place and setting their own hours. They also looked forward to enjoying the outdoors, something their professional lives allowed little time for. In fact, during my childhood they were only able to take one week off together each year, which we spent camping in the area they were now retiring to.

I looked forward to spending my last summer before college with my friends, but my parents wanted me to move with them and help remodel the store, an endeavor that would be ongoing throughout the first year they were in business. Following several heated arguments, we reached an agreement: I would spend the weekdays helping out at the store and return to the city for weekends with my friends. The drive wasn't much more than an hour, and I'd just bought my first car, so I wasn't as put out as I may have acted. Truth be told, I now treasure the memories of working with Mom and Dad that year.

The first task was to give the place a thorough cleaning, something requiring a couple days and more than a few gallons of bleach. After a morning of silent scrubbing, I decided to take a break and snoop around the back-office area, where I discovered a stereo system propped up on a rickety wood shelf in the corner. It was one of those old 70s units; a combination radio, record and 8-track player, but it worked. I was happy to have some music to break up the monotony of the task at hand, even though the only station it received played a static-filled mix of 70s and 80s country.

When I got back to scrubbing down the old soda fridge, the radio faded into loud static, something I quickly learned to tolerate, as the signal came from some distance away. The next time this happened, the crackle was interrupted by a broken-up woman's voice saying, "Carla is here." The radio then went back to static, followed by the sound of a twangy guitar as the music returned. I didn't pay much mind to this, as I assumed a different station cut in on that frequency, something not uncommon on older radios.

As promised, my parents let me go back to the city for the weekend, which quickly turned into Sunday afternoon and my time to drive back to the lake. I returned to the store to find it empty. Mom and Dad had wandered into the village, leaving boxes spread out in front of shelving units, needing to be stocked prior to opening for business. I decided to surprise them by getting an early start on filling the displays, so after turning the old radio up, I went to work.

As the sun began to set, the store became gloomy. New light fixtures were being installed that week, but until then the room was poorly lit by dim bulbs. I decided it was time to head upstairs. As I walked back to turn off the radio, it crackled to static, but once again was broken up by a woman's voice: "Carla came back." Every hair on my neck stood up as I heard the voice saying the same name through the crackling static of the radio. I couldn't get out of that building fast enough!

When the tourist season kicked in and the store was finally open, my parents needed my help more than ever. My trips back to the city were cut to every other weekend, but I didn't care; I was having a great time with the summer crowd that populated the resorts and campgrounds during the hot months.

Before I knew it, August was almost over, and it was time for me to pack up and head to college. I spent most of my last day at the store talking with my mom, listening to her parental warnings and advice she felt I needed to hear before being on my own. As we were having our heart-to-heart, Dad strolled in through the front accompanied by a man I'd never seen before but could tell Mom recognized.

"Mr. Wilson," she greeted the older gentleman, "what do you think of your old place?"

I realized this was the Mr. Wilson my parents had bought the store from, who now lived somewhere in Florida.

After exchanging pleasantries with Mom, the old man turned and locked his gaze on me, making me quite uncomfortable.

"This is our daughter, Karen," Mom said, making my introduction.

"Well, sorry for staring, young lady, but you look exactly like my sister did when she was young. For a minute, I thought I was seeing a ghost!"

"Did your sister also work here?" Dad asked.

"Oh, yes, Carla and I both spent our summers helping the folks out during the busy season."

I froze at the mention of that name. "Your sister's name was Carla?" I asked.

"Still is" replied Mr. Wilson. "Just visited her on my way up here. She lives in Georgia now. She hasn't been back to Ohio since our parents passed."

After checking out the store, my father walked Mr. Wilson out to his car. As soon as they had left the room, I told my mom about the voice coming through the radio mentioning Carla and how bizarre it was to find out I closely resembled someone by that name who had also worked in this store. "I'm sure it's just a coincidence" was all Mom would say about the matter, but I could tell she was also a bit spooked.

The next week, I moved away for my first year of college. When I returned for a visit that fall I asked my mom, half-jokingly, if anything else strange had happened. After a brief hesitation, she answered," Of course not," in a less than convincing tone. I went downstairs to see my dad, who was still working the counter. I noticed new speakers mounted in the corners, and the clear sound of pop music playing. I asked Dad what he'd done with the old stereo. "Your mother unhooked it one day and demanded I replace it. Right in the middle of a busy Saturday, can you believe that?" I could.

And Then There Was One

Hey, Guys! First, let me say, I LOVE The Creaking Door Podcast. You interview the best people in the biz, and you can tell you have personal relationships with many of them in the style of interview and the laid-back approach. Keep up the great work!

So I wanted to share a story with you guys that happened when I was just a child but is backed up by photos taken by my mom. We grew up in the city of Detroit, in a very impoverished community. My parents worked hard in their respective jobs. Dad was a janitor at a local plant, and Mom worked at a neighborhood diner. Even though we didn't have a lot of money and the toys that so many kids are used to growing up with, my parents always made sure I was still happy and having fun!

There were a couple of city parks where they would take me to play, and I loved being outside on the swings, slides, monkey bars, you name it. It was where I was happiest. Of the two parks, though, I most enjoyed the one farthest from the house. It was about a half-hour ride, but the park was bigger, closer to the water, and had more swings and slides. Most of all, my friends Stacia and Elise were always there. It never mattered what day or time I was there; they were still there when I showed up. I was eight years old, and they were eight-year-old twin sisters from another part of town. They did not go to my school; the only time we would see each other would be at the park.

We loved the swings most! We would always have competitions to see who could go the highest. They always seem to win, but we had so much fun. I am smiling right now, writing this to you, remembering how happy I was in those days. I guess, looking back on it now, it is peculiar that they were always there, and that I never saw a parent, ever. Because we lived far enough away to necessitate driving, my mom and dad were always with me. I always figured Stacia and Elise were within walking distance, and that's why their parents were never there. Whenever my parents yelled for me to come, I knew it was time to go home. Stacia and Elise would stand side by side and watch me leave. They never waved or said goodbye. They just stood there and watched me go.

There was a period where we were unable to go to my favorite playground, making me miss my time with Stacia and Elise. One day, I remember asking my mom when we could go back. She asked why I wanted to return to that particular park and why I wasn't happy at the one closer to home. I explained how much I enjoyed my time with my two friends at the park, and that they never came to the one closer to our home. I can remember the look on her face when I said that. She then asked about my friends at the park, so I told her about Stacia and Elise, my friends who were twin sisters and that because they didn't go to my school the only time I could see them was at the other playground.

Even as an eight-year-old, I remember finding it strange that she asked me so many questions about the sisters, as if she had never seen them before. She kept on with the questions, asking about the clothes they wore, how their hair was, how tall they were, who was the most outgoing. I remember all of those questions and thinking to myself how strange it was that she was asking me all this. I finally asked her why? I questioned why she didn't see all of this while we were playing. I will never forget her response, which to a child, didn't make sense, but now…. Yah, it makes a lot of sense. She said, "Devin, we stopped taking you to that playground because you never played with children. You just seemed to always be by yourself, swinging on the swing, and not playing with anyone else. That's why we stopped going there. You play with other children at the park closer to home."

I remember being confused about what she was saying to me. Finally, after many weeks of asking and starting to argue about it, my parents brought me back to that playground on a Saturday afternoon. As we pulled up, I saw Stacia and Elise on the swing set. I remember being so excited and as soon as we parked, I didn't give my parents a moment to say a word. I opened the door and ran right to the swing set, jumped on my favorite swing, and began the day with my friends whom I hadn't seen in so long. We swung for what seemed all day to an eight-year-old. I remember them asking me where I had been, and that they missed playing with me. I explained the best way a boy my age could what I comprehended from my talk with my mom, and the battles that ensued, to get me back to the park.

Finally, I heard my dad's voice yell, "Devin, it's getting late; time to go home, son." His forever call for me when they brought me to the park. As I got off the swing and was saying goodbye, I heard my mom say, "Devin, stand with your friends so I can get a picture of the three of you." I laugh about it now, knowing what she was doing, but Mom never brought a camera to the park or took pictures of me playing with friends. But I stood next to my friends, and Mom took the picture. Then I said my goodbyes to them and ran to the car. I remember looking back, and just like every time before, they just stood there and watched me; no waves, no emotion, just stood there.

Those strange moments of goodbye were something that finally resonated with me when I was an adult, and my mom shared the story with me. The year of that final time at the park with the sisters, my dad lost his job. After that school year ended, the family packed up and we moved to the west side of the state, toward Grand Rapids, where we had family. Mom and Dad found new jobs, and our lives changed for the better after moving. As a child, I never returned to the Detroit area or the park that I had loved so much.

Let's fast forward many years, and now I have just graduated from Western Michigan University and returned home to live with Mom and Dad, while I searched for my first career job. One night, Mom and I were sitting around the kitchen table, and somehow the topic of those days at the park with the twin sisters came up. After some discussion, I shared with her that now as an adult, there was something weird about those two. Amazing how the mind of an eight-year-old and an adult can sure see things differently. After I made that statement, she looked at me and said she had something to show me. She was never sure if she was going to share this with me, but if the opportunity presented itself, she would. This night was that night.

She went into the living room, opened a coffee table drawer, and from under a stack of papers pulled out two photos. The first photo she shared with me was the one in which she asked me to pose with my friends that day before we left the park. I had completely forgotten about this picture until that moment. She handed me the photograph, and all I could do was stare. There, in the photo, was me standing by the swing set, alone; just me, with no twin sisters standing next to me. The second photo she handed me was one, she explained, that she took earlier in the day of me on the swings with Stacia and Elise. The swing set had four swings. My favorite was always the one closest to the left. Stacia would take the second one in next to me, and Elise always chose the one next to her sister. In the photo you can see me swinging forward as high as I could get it. The two swings next to me were also in motion. The swing that Stacia was always in was swinging forward with me, and the next swing where Elise was, was swinging backward. But in the photo, the only person seen sitting in the swing was me.

Mom explained to me that those swings would always move when I was swinging at that park, but she always thought the empty swings were moving only because I was swinging. She said Dad never noticed a thing because he was forever reading the newspaper or a book he brought with him. She said she wrote off my "friends" as imaginary when I first told her about them, but as I fought with her more and more about getting back to the park, she started to think about it, and that's what prompted her to grab the camera. Even though I was raised in a strict Christian home, Mom always had that spiritual/paranormal side to her that she kept hidden, for the most part, from the family.

To this day, I still can't wrap my head around what I experienced as a child. To me, Stacia and Elise were my friends, and they were as real as you and me. I still think about them often, wondering if they are still there playing and if they have a new friend.

Night at the Cabin

Hi, Creaking Door, my name's Brian and I live in Duluth, Minnesota. I have to start this off by admitting something: I've never listened to your show. Sorry, just wanted you to know I've always been more of a non-believer when it comes to ghosts. My wife, on the other hand, is a big fan of the paranormal. She's met you both at events you've spoken at and pushed me to write you, hoping to get your insight on something that happened to me a few years ago.

It was the first week of December, and my wife had left with her mother and sister for their annual Christmas shopping trip to the Mall of America. It was before our son was born, so I was alone for the weekend. When I arrived at work Friday morning, I was informed that there was an electrical issue in my office, and I didn't need to stick around if I didn't want to. It was a sunny day and warmer than usual for that time of year, so I didn't have to think twice; I was out of there!

My father and some friends own a rustic hunting cabin about an hour outside of the city, and with the weather looking perfect for the weekend, I knew where I wanted to spend my free time. Deer season had just ended, so I'd have the place to myself. I'm not much of a hunter, but I love hiking in the woods, especially in the autumn when the leaves cover the forest floor. There's a crisp, damp smell to the air that takes me back to my childhood when Dad and I would spend the day walking those trails, exploring the natural beauty of the northern forest, memories I'll always cherish.

I hurried home, threw some clothes in a bag, filled the cooler with essentials (mainly burger and beer), and was on the road before noon. When I arrived, everything was exactly as I'd hoped it would be. The place was empty, and there were no cars at any of the cabins I'd passed on the road in. I had the forest to myself.

After making up a bunk and starting a fire in the woodstove to heat the place, I grabbed a book and headed out for a hike. There's a clearing on the property where I love to sit and read, which is exactly how I spent much of the afternoon. At some point, the fresh air and sunshine did me in, and I dozed off. When I woke, the sun was starting to set, so I headed back to the cabin, as it's very easy to get turned around in the woods once it's dark. This entire time, I didn't see or hear another person. I really felt like the entire forest belonged to me.

First thing I did when I got back was to throw some kindling and logs into the fire pit and got a small blaze going. I ate my dinner, cleaned the dishes, and settled in front of the fire with my radio and a cold beer, thoroughly enjoying the solitude.

Once again, the fresh air started to work its magic. Between that and the crackling of the burning wood, I found myself nodding off as a light snow began to fall on the woods. I extinguished the fire, visited the outhouse (did I mention this was a rustic place?), threw another log into the woodstove, and got ready to hit the bunk for the night.

I don't know why I bothered bringing my phone with me, as there was absolutely no reception in the area at that time. It was still the days of flip phones, and it was my first to have a camera in it, so I guess I was carrying it everywhere for that feature. The last thing I did before crawling between the sheets was plug it in to charge for the night.

When I woke the next morning, the sun was already up. Between the stillness of the cabin and the heat from the fire still burning in the woodstove, I really didn't want to get out of bed, but nature was calling. As I headed into the main lodge just outside the bunkroom, my eyes were drawn to the kitchen area. When I went to bed, my phone had been plugged into a socket on the opposite side of the room; but there it sat, flipped open on the dining table.

I immediately searched the cabin (not hard to do, since it's only two rooms) to make sure there wasn't an intruder. I proceeded to grab a shotgun and went outside to check the yard; aside from a light dusting of snow, all was as it had been the night before. As I headed back inside, it struck me: besides my footprints, the snow on the porch was undisturbed. Nobody had come in or out of the place that night.

After a few minutes in confused thought, I rationalized that I must have been sleep walking and moved the phone myself. What else could it be? Convinced it was just that, I made breakfast and looked forward to another day in the woods and a good long hike.

As I sat down to eat, I grabbed the phone to check the battery level when I noticed the camera had been used. Flipping to the gallery, I expected to see a picture of my thumb or the floor, whatever I may have sleepily snapped last night. I really wish that was the case, because what I saw scared the hell out of me!

There on the screen was the black shadow of a man, and when I say black, I mean pitch black. You couldn't see anything through this thing. The shadow spread across the floor of the lodge, obviously cast by whoever or whatever took the picture. In the background was the open door to the bunkroom, and me asleep in bed!

I quickly grabbed my things, threw the breakfast dishes in the sink, and got the hell out of there! The entire ride home, I tried to rationalize what had happened. I'd been going to that place my entire life, and never had anything like this happened!

I couldn't bring myself to tell my dad about the occurrence, even when he asked for an explanation as to why dirty dishes were left in the sink; a crime by camp standards, as it attracts mice and bugs. He was also thrown off the following fall when I had an excuse every weekend he invited me to go to the camp, something I'd never turned down in the past.

The next year I worked up my courage and returned and have done so every year since. Although it was a couple years before I'd spend the night again, I'm now fine staying for the weekend, and have started bringing my son along as well. Nothing odd happened after that night, but I cringe a bit every time I pull up that dirt drive, thinking "What if this is the day he comes back?" I still don't believe in ghosts, but I find myself a lot more open minded after that night.

Stump-Jumpers

Tim and Brad, I love your show and was I ever surprised to find out you guys are Yoopers! My name is Laura, and I live in Chicago now, but grew up in Grand Rapids, Michigan, and spent a lot of time in the Upper Peninsula. I wanted to pass along this story from my childhood, as it happened right in your backyard.

My grandparents owned a home near Brimley, Michigan, right on the shore of Lake Superior. They both passed when I was young, but my mother's family decided rather than sell the house, they'd keep it to use as a vacation property. The location was perfect for recreation, as we had our own waterfront to swim and play at during the summer and it was near a trail my dad and uncles used for snowmobiling in the winter. Any time of the year my parents could get away, we headed for Brimley.

I loved spending time there with my cousins, especially Lisa and Cliff, who were closest in age to me. Of my mom's family, they lived nearest the house, a little over an hour away in Munising, Michigan, and always joined us when we went up north. I've often considered writing a book about our adventures there as kids, as there were some doozies, but the following account is the only time one of those adventures left us trembling.

It happened in the summer of 1978. My Aunt Andrea, Mom's youngest sister, was getting divorced. Her soon-to-be ex was keeping the house, and instead of looking for a new place right away, she decided to live at the vacation property for the summer. Mom and my Aunt Sally (Lisa and Cliff's mother) arranged to spend the month of July with her to lend moral support and help her get back on her feet. Mom let me come along, and although Lisa and Cliff weren't there the whole time, their dad brought them over every Thursday to spend the weekends.

Lisa and I were 13, and Cliff turned 15 that month. Though she and I were starting to become "girly," whenever we got together in the summer, we transformed back into the tomboys we'd grown up as. Cliff was a big outdoorsman and loved taking us out in the woods to explore, pointing out the names of plants and what animal a certain pile of scat came from; just what every young girl wants to know! It may sound boring to kids in today's world but exploring the forest and hanging out on the beach were the things I loved to do most.

One Saturday, when Aunt Andrea was feeling particularly low, Mom and Sally decided to take her for a girl's night out. They were going across the border to Sault Ste. Marie, Ontario, for dinner and a movie, and weren't planning on being back early. We were left to fend for ourselves with only one rule from the parents: Don't get into any trouble!

As soon as they backed out of the driveway, the plotting and scheming began. Down the road about a mile was a dirt road that nobody lived on; just a few abandoned houses and one cabin, which was used only during the fall by hunters. We knew this, because at one time or another, we'd "visited" each of these places while out exploring. Although most of the structures appeared ready to fall in, one was more recently abandoned and still had an old stove and fridge in the kitchen, and some worn through furnishings in the living room. This was dubbed the *Haunted House*, because it fit the Hollywood stereotype of what a ghost-infested home should look like: peeling paint, broken windows, and an overgrown yard with no other structures in sight.

As we grilled hot dogs over a fire on the beach, Lisa unveiled her plan for the evening. While cleaning out the garage with her dad in the spring, she'd found an old Ouija board in the rafters, which she was dying to try out. The three of us, along with Cliff's friend Jeremy, a boy around his age who spent summers at a cabin down the beach, would take the board to the haunted house for an improvised séance. What could possibly go wrong?

I was a little scared at the thought of using the Ouija, and I could tell Cliff was apprehensive, although he wouldn't dare say so in front of Jeremy, but Lisa had a one track mind and once it was made up, there was no turning back. After dinner, we threw on sweatshirts and jeans (more for fending off mosquitos than the cold), retrieved the board from the garage, and headed down the road.

Since the sight of four teenagers walking down the road with an Ouija board might arouse suspicions, we decided to take a path through the woods. Aside from avoiding adults, the trail was a shorter route, and one we knew well. It was mid-summer, so we still had a couple hours of sunlight left; plenty of time to get to the house, summon the dead, and make our way back in time to roast marshmallows on the beach.

We entered the house through the back door, which opened into the kitchen, and determined the living room would be best for the session. It had the remains of some furniture and was close enough to the entrance that we could beat a hasty retreat should things go badly.

We set the board up on the bare wood floor in the middle of the dusty room, as Cliff and I agreed to attempt first contact. Placing our fingers on the planchette, we began to question the Ouija: Is anyone here? What's your name? When did you die? The planchette remained motionless. After a few minutes of this, Cliff began to joke, and our unsuccessful attempt at communication came to an end.

I don't know if Lisa and Jeremy were more open to the spirit world, or if Lisa's summertime crush on him caused her to subconsciously move the planchette, but as soon as their turn started, that thing was all over the place, and answered almost every question they put forth. After some time of this, Cliff, who was a little freaked out, mentioned we should get moving if we wanted to be back before dark. Though Lisa disagreed, we said goodbye to the spirits and packed the board away.

We left the house and started back down the path, a bit apprehensive to be entering the woods after what may have been a long conversation with the other side, but it was still light out and the mood softened when we all started cracking jokes and poking fun at Cliff over his rush to end the séance. We still had a beachfront fire to look forward to, free of adult supervision, so at that point, I thought our night was just beginning.

As we exited the dense forest into a clearing that marked the halfway point of the trail, I literally ran into Lisa as the others stopped dead in their tracks. Standing at the edge of the tree line, just feet from us, was this… thing! It couldn't have been more than four feet tall. Its face was awful; it had a small, snout-like nose, slightly protruding jaw with an underbite that showed two short tusks or fangs sticking up, and short, pointed ears on the sides of the head, but closer to the top than a human's. The eyes were yellow, and it seemed to be squinting, so I couldn't tell how wide they were. The ribcage protruded somewhat, and it was covered in short, brown fur, darker than that of a whitetail deer. The thing's feet and lower legs were in the tall grass, so I didn't get a look at them, but the upper legs looked very muscular. The arms seemed longer than they should have been, and the fingers ended in either long nails or claws.

It took one step toward us, and Lisa let out a blood-curdling scream as she hurled the Ouija at it. We were gone! I don't remember anything about the run back, but when I got to the road, I was alone, sure the monster had picked off the others one by one! A few seconds later, I heard crashing through the trees, and Cliff, followed by the others, emerged from the woods.

Feeling safer on the road, we briskly walked back to the house. The bonfire was put on hold until we noticed a fire going at the neighbor's. Being alone outdoors was the last thing any of us wanted at this point, and even with others on the beach, we called it an early night and locked ourselves inside way before our mothers returned.

The next day, accompanied by a couple boys from the area, Cliff and Jeremy returned to the field to collect the Ouija board. When they described the encounter to the local kids, one of them said his uncle had a run-in with one of these creatures at a nearby state park years back. Locals referred to them as Stump-Jumpers, supposedly due to their size, speed, and leaping abilities. He said that the creatures are usually reported in yards or fields that border the woodlands, and they have a fear of humans.

They may be afraid of people, but this thing wasn't the one running and screaming the day we saw it! Its face is burned into my mind, and I've never forgotten that night. I never went back down that trail again.

My mother is approaching 80 now, but every summer she and I try to make it to the U.P. to meet Lisa and Aunt Sally at the family house for a few days. Lisa, who still lives near Munising, called a few weeks ago to plan for the annual getaway and before we got off the phone, told me a story she'd heard at work. A co-worker was on the way home when something crossed the rural road in front of him. He thought it was a young Bigfoot, but the description he gave sounded exactly like the Stump-Jumper we ran into that day! We both agreed, if these things are roaming the Upper Peninsula forests, we'll stick to the beaches.

The Road Less Traveled

Hello, Guys! Long time listener and a first-time submitter of a story for your show. My name is Danielle, from a small community on the shores of Lake Michigan in Wisconsin. The story I am about to share with you and your listeners is a story I have been unwilling to share with a lot of people, until now. Hearing other experiences shared on your show has allowed me to sit down and type this out.

This happened over 40 years ago. I was just seventeen years old and still relatively new being behind the wheel of a car and cruising the roads of our small town. I started working at my parents' hardware store when I was just fourteen years old, probably breaking some age-related working laws, but when your parents own the store, I guess you get those privileges.

From the moment I started working, I was putting money away to be able to purchase my vehicle as soon as I was old enough to drive. I couldn't wait to be ready to jump behind the wheel and go where and when I wanted. It was a freedom my older sister was not afforded when she was of legal age to drive, since not a single penny for a car was saved while she was working at the hardware store. I would have a front-row seat as she was relegated to begging my parents to borrow their vehicle, a battle she would often lose. That was not how I wanted to spend my early years of being able to drive.

I remember this particular night like it happened yesterday. Events, sights, sounds, even smells are forever a part of me and things I will never forget. It was a beautiful, hot summer night, where the windows were rolled down, the music was louder than my singing, and life was perfect. These kinds of summer nights, growing up in Wisconsin, are some of my favorite memories. I was driving along on one of the many back roads that have trees covering each side, and are so dense they almost block the moonlight. That's when I saw.... her. She looked like someone who was my age, on the side of the road waving me down in my headlights. She didn't look scared or like she had been hurt, but coming from a small town where everyone knows everyone, I certainly did not recognize her, so if she was a tourist, I wanted to make sure she was all right.

I slowed my car, pulled to the shoulder of the road, and slowly rolled the car to a stop just in front of her. Now I know what you must be thinking "Why would a seventeen-year-old girl pull over and see if a stranger was OK?" I ask myself that every time this memory is brought back to me. I mean, I never would have pulled over for a strange, older person, but since this girl was my age, the threat was not there, not yet. She approached the passenger side of my car and I rolled down the window. She seemed very thankful for me stopping, and I remember her having a pleasant smile, but it was also the eyes that I remember very vividly. At the time, I had no idea why, but now, after a lifetime of thinking and rethinking and analyzing this night, the only word I can come up with to describe them is "dead"!

She said she was visiting our town and staying at a family cabin in the area. It was now dark, and she didn't like being alone on the road because of the wildlife in the area. She was hoping to find a lift, so I politely offered her the ride she was wanting. Her eyes were the first thing that stood out to me. Two more events were about to happen that I can't shake even to this day. She got into the front passenger seat and we were off down the road. As I had stated before, it was a hot summer Wisconsin night, so my windows were down. She immediately asked if I could roll up the windows; she was freezing. As strange as I found that, I politely rolled up the windows. I thought maybe being outside for her walk, she had simply caught a chill. That was my rationalization anyway.

She said the cabin was just a few miles up the road, and couldn't thank me enough for the ride. Beyond that, it was hard to keep a conversation going. With the windows being up (I was afraid to turn on the vent because she said she was so chilled), the air in the car was getting stagnant, and that's when I noticed the third thing that stands out from that night; the smell. It became very noticeable; a heavy perfume smell. Underneath that, it seemed there was a more substantial odor that the perfume was meant to cover up, but I couldn't put a finger on what that was.

We drove for about five minutes when she said we were coming up to the road to get to her family cabin. When we approached the turn, it was an old two-track I had driven by hundreds of times but never had a reason to take. The day before, we had a huge thunderstorm roll through the area that drenched us with an entire day of rain. I felt a little uncomfortable taking my small car too far down the old two-track, knowing how wet and muddy it would be. I went as far as I felt comfortable down the old path and explained to her that this was as far as I could go. She thanked me for the ride and got out of the car. It was at this moment that my life changed forever!

Before she shut the door, she turned and looked at me and said, "Don't ever walk these roads alone at night." The pleasant smile she had when I first pulled over to pick her up was gone. Her mouth was now part of the saddest face I have ever seen, fitting perfectly with those dead eyes. Next, she just turned and walked down the path, not even shutting the door to my car. For a moment, I just sat there stunned, and watched her walk down the trail as far as my headlights would reach. Once she was beyond my lights I snapped out of it, and a chill ran down my body as I reached across the front seat and slammed the passenger door shut. Sitting there on that dark, two-track road, fear overtook me, and I threw my headlights to bright to give me more visibility, as I needed to back out as quickly as I could. Once the brights were on, I saw it: farther down the road, the old sign read, "St. Anthony's Cemetery." To this day, I don't know how I did not end up putting my car into a tree backing out of the old road, but somehow I found myself back on the main road and driving as fast as I could.

I drove for a bit before the shock wore off and then I started crying uncontrollably. I was shaking, but I couldn't stop until I reached a city street with activity and more lights. When I finally got to the town, I pulled into a parking lot, opened the door and got out of that car as fast as I could. Before I knew it, I was on the ground getting sick, and all I could smell was "that smell" that I was noticing in the car. I finally collected myself and tried to piece it all together. NOTHING made sense when I tried to rationalize the events that happened just moments ago.

It seemed like forever, sitting there and trying to collect my thoughts. I finally made my way home where my mom was sitting in the kitchen as I came in, and immediately she knew something was wrong. She ran to me and gave me a hug; I needed that more than anything at that moment. It was the most real thing I had felt in the past few hours. Once again, I broke down in tears, this time in my mother's arms, and so began the rest of the evening, trying to explain to her what happened and somehow make sense of it all.

She explained to me that St. Anthony's Cemetery was an old cemetery run by the local Catholic parish many, many years ago. It had been abandoned for new burials long ago but was being looked after by a charity group for the local Catholic churches. As far as the girl on the road, she would remain a mystery for another twenty years.

I could never drive that car again. The "smell" would never leave it. I traded it in shortly after and embraced my new car. As for my summertime, after the sun went down, back road cruises, well, those came to an end as well. To this day, I do not like to be on the road after dark, and I never went by that old two-track road again. For many years I was seeing professional help to get me through this event, but no matter how hard I try, certain parts of that night will never leave me. Whoever that young lady was, she will forever haunt me.

Twenty years after the event, there was a day I was finally able to sit down and do some historical research on my hometown. What I found has helped me to piece some of my night together, but only deepens the haunting of that night. In 1954, a sixteen-year-old girl, by the name of Adrianna, was killed on that very road from a bear attack. She was visiting her family at their summer cabin and was out walking that very road when the attack happened. Officials were shocked about a bear attack and could only surmise the family's small dog triggered something in the bear to approach. The dog survived and returned home without Adrianna, and that's how the family was alerted to something being wrong. They believe the young girl panicked and ran, which provoked the bear to pursue.

I know there are "Phantom Hitchhiker" stories all over the place, but those stories have multiple "witnesses" and numerous people who have experienced the phantom hitchhiker of their area. My event, as far as I know, is a one and done! There was NO legend in our area of the girl you should not pick up late at night on a dark county road. I know what I experienced that night. It was real and life changing to this very day. Her words, I will never forget, "Don't ever walk these roads alone at night."

I don't know why it happened to me or why I was the one to experience that moment. What I do know, or at least believe, is that Adrianna was in my car, and instead of bringing her to her family cabin, I brought her back to her final resting place. I have not, nor do I ever think I will go to that cemetery to see if an Adrianna is buried there. I don't think I have to. I know what happened that night.

Afterword

By Brad Blair and Tim Ellis

Growing up in Michigan's Upper Peninsula, every day brought a different adventure. We might be exploring the shoreline of the St. Mary's River, on the lookout for lake monsters, trudging through the forest, certain that the sound of every breaking twig was a lurking sasquatch, or riding our bikes down country roads in search of abandoned dwellings that might house the spirits of past inhabitants. Those were the days before modern video gaming when kids played outside all day and into the night, dreading the sound of mom's voice breaking through the darkness to announce it was time to come inside.

We consider ourselves lucky to have grown up in those days. Luckier yet to have done so in Michigan's U.P., an area of land that comprises roughly one-third of the state yet is inhabited by only three percent of its population. Where being in the center of downtown is only mere minutes from lakefront or woodlands, where the day's activities are limited only by the depths of the imagination. Imagination is one thing we had plenty of back in those days, and we kept it fueled by regular trips to the library to check out books on ghosts, cryptids, UFOs, and many other topics which our parents and many of our peers considered fantastic and strange.

Afterword

As related in this book, many habitats throughout the Great Lakes region offer similar surroundings and more than a few uncanny creatures and legends, some found throughout North America, others distinct to the area. At one time or another, Tim, and I, along with the rest of our team, the Upper Peninsula Paranormal Research Society, have studied and investigated nearly all the creatures appearing in these pages. We have done extensive reading on the legends that have added colorful tales to the lands and waters that make up this unique corner of the globe.

Creating this book has motivated us to continue our research into the phenomena that we document within these pages. Our work has taken us down strange and sometimes shocking roads, both literally and figuratively. We have been amazed by what has taken place within the Great Lakes region.

Some of these stories were familiar to us. Others we had heard only in bits and pieces. There were brand new stories that left us feeling like children around a campfire, spellbound and looking over our shoulders as chills slowly crawled up our spines.

We hope you've enjoyed this peek inside the strange and sometimes frightening, fantastic tales from the place we call home.

If you are a resident of or are ever fortunate enough to visit this region, keep a keen eye on your surroundings; between the dark forests and the unexplored depths of its waterways, the Great Lakes Basin indeed hides more mysteries yearning to be discovered.

About the Authors

Adventurer, researcher, and public speaker Brad Blair has harbored a passion for the strange and unusual since childhood. Growing up in Michigan's Upper Peninsula, Brad spent his days exploring regional legends and folklore, reading about cryptid creatures, UFOs, psychic phenomena, and his favorite topic – ghosts and hauntings.

Brad has explored haunted locations throughout North America and beyond, has contributed to many publications and documentaries on the paranormal and continues to pursue a lifelong study of the bizarre.

He is a founding member of the Upper Peninsula Paranormal Research Society, Co-host of *Creaking Door Paranormal Radio*, and co-founder of the *Michigan Paranormal Convention*.

Brad lives in Sault Ste. Marie, Michigan, with his wife Jennifer and son Kaden. He owns and operates several tourism-related businesses.

****

Tim Ellis is married and the father of three fur babies in beautiful Sault Ste. Marie, Michigan, where he was born and raised. He and his wife, Lindsay, own a radio station, Eagle 95.1 WUPN, where he is the Morning Show Host. In 1998, along with two childhood friends Brad Blair and Steve LaPlaunt, they started the journey that became The Upper Peninsula Paranormal Research Society "Yoopers" (U.P.P.R.S.). 2000 to 2006, Tim took his love of radio and ghosts as a Co-Host for a podcast called TAPS Family Radio, a wildly popular TAPS team branch from the Ghost Hunters T.V. show. In 2008, Tim and Brad Co-Founded, with the support of their U.P.P.R.S. team, The Michigan Paranormal Convention, becoming one of the largest Paranormal Gatherings in the United States to date. In 2012, Tim brought back his love of radio and ghosts when he and Brad created "Creaking Door Paranormal Radio" podcast, on all the major platforms such as iTunes, Google Play, Stitcher, and Spotify.

In 2018, Tim, Steve, and Brad worked together again as they tri-authored their first book, *Yoopernatural Haunts: From The Case Files of The Upper Peninsula Paranormal Research Society*. The book went to number one, multiple times, on Amazon's New Releases; Ghost & Hauntings. Tim continues to be a veteran paranormal investigator, working in the field for over two decades. He is featured in numerous publications, including *U.S.A. Today*, *The Detroit Free Press*, and *Lake Superior Magazine*, to name a few and helped in several documentaries on the paranormal. As much as he loves radio, Tim is truly happiest when working, writing, and speaking about ghosts, monsters, legends, and everything that keeps most people up at night.

Bibliography

Bishop, Hugh. *Haunted Lake Superior.* Duluth, MN: Lake Superior Port Cities, Inc., 2003.

Black, Bela. "Haunted Presque Isle Lighthouse." American Ghost Stories. June 14, 2009, https://americanghoststories.com/haunted-places/haunted-lighthouses-presque-isle-lighthouse-michigan.

Butts, Ed. *Shipwrecks, Monsters, and Mysteries of the Great Lakes.* Toronto, Ontario: Tundra Books, 2010.

Carlson, John. "Rocks, Ghosts, Magic Forest in the U.P." *Detroit Free Press,* September 25, 2014.

Cassady, Charles Jr. *Paranormal Great Lakes.* Atglen, PA: Schiffer Publishing, 2009.

Clements, Todd. *Haunts of Mackinac: The Next Chapter.* Grosse Point, MI: House of Hawthorne Publishing, 2016.

Coleman, Loren. *Mothman.* New York, NY: Paraview Press, 2002.

Curwood, James. *The Great Lakes.* New York, NY: The Knickerbocker Press, 1909.

Duco, Jennifer. Interview with Brad Blair. Personal Interview. Sault Ste. Marie, MI, March 2, 2020.

Durr, Matt. "Video Captures 'Sea Monster' Swimming Near Pier in South Haven." MLive. July 3, 2019. https://www.mlive.com/news/2019/07/video-captures-sea-monster-swimming-near-pier-in-south-haven.html

Fischer, Marilyn. *Spirits at Seul Choix Pointe.* Gulliver, MI: Seul Choix Press, 2013.

Foreman, Laura. *Haunted Holidays: Discovery Travel Adventures.* Maspeth, NY: Langenschiedt Publishers, Inc., 1999.

Franklin, Dixie. *Haunts of the Upper Great Lakes.* Grand Rapids, MI: Thunder Bay Press, 1977.

Freeborn, B.L. "The Newberry Tablet: A New Way to Read It." NoahSage. August 2, 2015. https://noahsage.com/2015/08/02/the-newberry-tablet-a-new-way-to-read-it/

Godfrey, Linda. *American Monsters.* New York, NY: Penguin Group, 2014.

___*Haunted Wisconsin: Ghosts and Strange Phenomena of the Badger State.* Mechanicsburg, PA: Stackpole Books, 2010.

Godfrey, Linda and Shiel, Lisa. *Strange Michigan.* Madison, WI: Trails Books, 2008.

Gringhuis, Dirk. *Lore of the Great Turtle.* Mackinac Island, MI: Mackinac Island State Park Commission, 1970.

___ *Were-Wolves and Will-O-The Wisps.* Mackinac Island, MI: Mackinac Island State Park Commission, 1974.

Guiley, Rosemary Ellen. *The Encyclopedia of Ghosts and Spirits.* New York, NY: Facts on File, 1992.

Hamlin, Marie Caroline Watson. *Legends of Le Detroit.* London, England: Forgotten Books, 2017.

Hermanson, Don. *Ghost Hunting on Mackinac Island*. Houghton, MI: Keweenaw Video Productions, 2012

___ *Ghost Hunting With the UPPRS*. Houghton, MI: Keweenaw Video Productions, 2008.

Hollatz, Tom and Dwyer, Seal. *The Haunted Northwoods*. St. Cloud, MN: North Star Press, 2000.

Kennedy, Sequoyah. "Another Mothman Sighting Reported in Indiana." Mysterious Universe. February 5, 2019. https://mysteriousuniverse. org/2019/02/another-mothman-sighting-reported-in-indiana/indiana/.

Konkolesky, William. Interview with Tim Ellis. Personal Interview. Sault Ste. Marie, MI, February 3, 2020.

Mertz, Henrieta. "The Lost Gods and Tablet of Prehistoric Michigan." Ancient America. March 8, 2015. https://ancientamerica.com/ category/newberry-tablet/

Nesbitt, Mark and Wilson, Patty. *Haunted Pennsylvania: Ghosts and Strange Phenomena of the Keystone State*. Mechanicsburg, PA, Stackpole Books, 2006.

Norman, Michael. *Haunted Wisconsin*. Black Earth, WI: Trail Books, 2001.

Nute, Grace Lee. *The Voyageur*. New York, NY: D. Appleton & Co., 1931.

Offutt, Jason. "Backcountry Terror When Black-eyed Kids Turn Up." The Examiner. November 24, 2010. https://www.examiner.net/ article/20101124/NEWS/311249722.

Schlosser, S.E. *Spooky Pennsylvania: Tales of Hauntings, Strange Happenings, and Other Local Lore*. Guildord, CT: Morris Book Publishing LLC, 2007.

Schoolcraft, Henry. *The Hiawatha Legends*. Philadelphia, PA: J.B. Lippencott & Co., 1856.

Steiger, Brad and Steiger, Sherry. *Real Encounters, Different Dimensions, and Otherworldly Beings*. Canton, MI: Visible Ink Press, 2014.

Steingass, Dr. Sheanna. Interview with Brad Blair. Personal Interview. Sault Ste. Marie, MI, December 3, 2019.

Stonehouse, Frederick. *Haunted Lakes.* Duluth, MN: Lake Superior Port Cities, Inc., 1997.

_____. *Haunted Lakes II.* Duluth, MN: Lake Superior Port Cities, Inc., 2000.

Winfield, Mason. *Haunted Rochester: A Supernatural History of the Lower Genesee.* Chicago, IL: History Press, 2008.

Unknown. "American Sea Serpent in Lake Ontario." *Oswego Palladium*, July 1, 1833.

Unknown. "Lake Monster." *Kingston Gazette,* March 26, 1842.

Unknown. "Lake Serpent." Kingston Gazette, August 14, 1829.

Unknown. "Monster in Burlington Bay." *Kingston Daily News,* August 17, 1877

Made in the USA
Columbia, SC
17 July 2023

20158745R00093